Interpreting the Atonement

INTERPRETING THE ATONEMENT

by

ROBERT H. CULPEPPER

STEVENS BOOK PRESS

WAKE FOREST, NORTH CAROLINA

INTERPRETING THE ATONEMENT

Reprinted 1988

ISBN 0-913029-13-0

Library of Congress Catalog Card Number 66-22948

STEVENS BOOK PRESS
245 E. Roosevelt Ave.
P. O. Box 71, Wake Forest, N. C. 27587
Telephone 919-556-3830

To
my wife
Kay
and
my daughter
Cathy

Preface

This book was prepared with theological students in mind, but it is hoped that it will be of value to pastors and thoughtful laymen as well. No attempt is made to give out homiletical tidbits; rather the concern is for the theological understanding which underlies all preaching and Christian witness.

The effective communication of the gospel demands an intelligent understanding of the Christian message. Nothing is more central in this message than the good news of God's saving action in Jesus Christ. This message reaches its climax in the story of the death and resurrection of God's Son. This was the center of the *kerygma* (proclamation) of the earliest church as the sermons in Acts, the epistles of Paul, and the passion narrative in the gospels make clear.

The Bible concerns itself with a particular stream of history which reaches its climax in the Christ-event. This stream of history has its root in God's redemption of Israel from bondage in Egypt and his choice of her to be his own people; it has its fruit in God's redemption of the church and his choice of this people to have a servant ministry to the world. Standing between these two as the connecting link and the integrating center is the Christ-event, centering in the incarnation, life, death, and resurrection of the Son of God.

Christian faith dares to affirm that what happened to Jesus of Nazareth in ancient Palestine somewhere between 25 and 32 A.D. "did not happen in a corner," but that this particular stream of history is redemptive history with universal significance for all history. In the New Testament witness, event and interpretation are inseparably bound together. Interpretation

7

without event would be mythology. Event without interpretation would be "mere history." The two together in indissoluble union constitute salvation-history.

What is the biblical witness concerning this salvation-history? How does the death of Jesus differ from that of a martyr? How does the death of this one in an obscure city of the ancient world almost two thousand years ago have saving significance for me today? How has the atonement been interpreted in the history of the Christian church? How are we to interpret it today? It is to such questions as these that this study addresses itself.

There is no pretension of finality of statement in this study. I am quite aware of its many inadequacies. "Ah, but a man's reach should exceed his grasp, or what's a heaven for?"

There is also no claim to originality here. My deep indebtedness to the works of others should be evident as one consults the footnotes. I have tried to give credit where credit is due. Any omissions of this type that may exist are purely unintentional. All quotations from the Bible, unless otherwise specified, are from the Revised Standard Version.

Now it is my happy privilege to express gratitude to those who have been of particular help to me in the preparation of this book. Two faculty members of Southern Baptist Theological Seminary, Louisville, Kentucky, Dr. Wayne Ward and Dr. Eric Rust, read the manuscript when it was in an early, rough stage of preparation, giving encouragement and making helpful suggestions. Mrs. Naoko Abe typed the manuscript; Michiko Uesugi helped prepare the indexes. My missionary colleagues Mr. Calvin Parker, Miss Anita Coleman, and Dr. Tucker Callaway helped with proofreading. My wife also helped with the proofreading and gave understanding, love, and encouragement. None of these, however, must be held responsible for the deficiencies of the book. For these I must take full responsibility.

Working with the Wm. B. Eerdmans Publishing Company has been a pleasure. I am particularly grateful for the complete freedom which the publisher has given me.

ROBERT H. CULPEPPER

Fukuoka, Japan

Contents

Introduction

In Bunyan's immortal *Pilgrim's Progress* Christian embarks on his journey from the City of Destruction to the Celestial City carrying a heavy burden on his back. He bears this burden until he comes to a place where there stands a cross and a little below at the bottom of the hill a sepulchre. At the foot of the cross the burden rolls from his shoulders and tumbles down the hill until it is swallowed up in the empty tomb and seen no more. With fidelity to the biblical witness Bunyan accurately depicts the experience of Christians throughout the ages.

As Moses removed his shoes from his feet when he encountered God in the burning bush, spiritually speaking we would remove our shoes as we attempt to interpret the atonement, mindful that this is particularly "holy ground." Our approach is that of *fides quaerens intellectum,* "faith in search of understanding," to use Augustine's famous words. And yet reverence must not stifle questions, and intellectual honesty must not be sacrificed upon the altar of spiritual humility. Still, one must not expect the whole counsel of God laid bare and the ineffable mystery of divine grace adequately expressed in perishable human words.

The doctrine of the atonement is the Holy of Holies of Christian theology. It is a doctrine of unfathomable depth and inexhaustible mystery. Christian theology reaches its climax in it, and in a large measure it is determinative of all other doctrines. Theology is Christian only insofar as all of its doctrines are illuminated by the doctrine of the atonement.

The God of our salvation is the God who has revealed himself decisively in Jesus Christ. He is the God and Father of our Lord

11

Jesus Christ, the one who spared not his own Son but freely gave him up for us all (Rom. 8:32). Man is God's creature, but a lost creature in rebellion against his Creator and unable to save himself. No other doctrine so clearly reveals man's sinful state and his inability to save himself from it. The doctrine of the atonement reveals the nature of salvation as reconciliation, reconciliation to God and man, and the acceptance in life of the way of the cross. The atonement is not automatic, but requires from man a response, the response of repentance and faith. Through his saving act in Christ God creates a new Israel, a new people of God, the church. What God has already done for us in Christ is the solid basis of our hope concerning what he yet will do in the future.

"Atonement" is an ambiguous term which requires definition. It is of Anglo-Saxon origin and its original meaning is "at-one-ment" or reconciliation, the restoration of broken fellowship. In Shakespearean English to atone is to reconcile, and the one time the word "atonement" is used in the King James Version of the New Testament it has the meaning of reconciliation (Rom. 5:11). In its theological usage, however, the term "atonement" has acquired another meaning, that is, the means by which reconciliation between God and man is achieved, the cost of reconciliation to God. In general usage also the verb "to atone" has come to mean to make reparation or to make amends for an offense. As the latter meaning has come to the fore, the former meaning has receded into the background. The result is that dictionaries now generally list "reconciliation" as an archaic or obsolete meaning of the term "atonement."[1] In this study the term "atonement" is used in the sense of the saving action of God in Christ through which our reconciliation to God is effected. The emphasis is thus placed upon the means by which the salvation is achieved rather than upon the nature of the salvation thus secured. And the crucial question is this: how can the crucifixion of a man in the first century have any saving significance for my life today?

The doctrine of the atonement in Christian theology presupposes the biblical understanding of sin. But it is this very understanding of sin which is becoming increasingly foreign

[1] For a helpful discussion of the meaning of the term "atonement" consult Robert S. Paul, *The Atonement and the Sacraments* (London: Hodder and Stoughton, 1961), pp. 17-32.

to modern man. One of the legacies of the so-called enlighten-
ment was the exaltation of man. Man became the measure
of all things to such an extent as to evoke the parody on the
angels' song: "Glory to *man* in the highest!" The category of
evolution, first worked out in the biological realm, was applied
to every aspect of human existence. An optimistic view regarding progress as inevitable developed. "Every day in every way
I'm getting better and better." Science, education, and technology
held out almost infinite possibilities for social betterment and
for the construction of a utopia on earth. Sin came to be regarded as a relic of man's animal ancestry, a growing pain in
the development of the race, a "stepping stone to higher things."

It was World War I which burst this bubble of optimism; and
before it could form again came World War II, along with
prison camp atrocities and the extermination of six million
Jews. "Man's inhumanity to man" stood out in bold relief.
Never before had Kant's emphasis upon "radical evil" seemed
so relevant, not because of any basic change in human nature
but because man's progress in the moral and spiritual realm had
not kept pace with his technological advance, and because for
the first time man held within his hands the possibility of destroying not just millions of people, as in previous wars, but civilization itself. Moreover, the division of the world into two hostile camps, the cold war, and brush-fire wars, which at any
time might become an atomic holocaust, have given modern man
the sensation of sitting on a powder keg while children play with
matches nearby.

Still, the problem has been interpreted largely in horizontal
terms with the dimension of the vertical receiving relatively
little attention. True, theologians like Karl Barth, Emil Brunner, and Reinhold Niebuhr have emphasized sin as the assertion
of man's pride, the rebellion of the creature against the Creator.
Moreover, secular historians like Arnold Toynbee and evangelists
like Billy Graham have called attention to the sickness of contemporary civilization. Rudolf Bultmann has tried to explain
sin in terms of Heidegger's category of "inauthentic existence,"
and Paul Tillich has spoken of it in terms of "estrangement."

As man enters the space age and sees the realization of the
most fanciful dreams of other generations, the conquest of
other worlds does not seem as difficult as the conquest of this
one, and bridging the distance between the planets seems a less

arduous task than bridging the distance between man and his
fellow man. The real space problem lies not in the world without but in the world within, not in the distance between the
planets, but in the distance between man and his fellow man,
and ultimately in the distance between man and God.

In interpreting sin in terms of man's estrangement from God,
however, we have left the realm of that which is obvious to all
and are affirming that which is known only to faith on the
basis of revelation. Perhaps as never before modern man is
aware of an estrangement at the center of his existence. But
so secularized has Western culture become that the note of
sin as rebellion against a personal God has been virtually
drowned out, while the Eastern religions offer no theological
basis for such an understanding. But we reiterate our point.
The doctrine of the atonement in Christian theology can be
understood only against the background of a biblical understanding of sin.

Man is a sinner both by nature and by practice. Sin is basically
rebellion against God, the refusal to let God be God in one's
life. It is rooted in unbelief and expresses itself in pride, self-
seeking, sensuality, and in a multitude of antisocial attitudes
and acts. Sin estranges man from God, creating a barrier between the creature and the Creator. Likewise sin estranges a
man from his true self, creating a disharmony within the personality and enslaving the higher self to the lower self. Moreover, sin estranges a man from his fellow man. Sin expresses
itself in self-seeking, and the self-seeking interests of one individual or group inevitably run into conflict with the self-
seeking interests of another individual or group. The consciousness of estrangement caused by sin produces the anxiety of
guilt. This comes from the negative judgment of the conscience,
the judge within.[2] The sense of guilt expresses itself in the
fear of punishment and even in what the psychiatrists call the
need for punishment. Psychosomatic medicine has made us
conscious that a great number of physical disorders are rooted
in emotional problems, the sense of guilt being one of the chief
of these. Moreover, the sense of guilt entering the subconscious
often produces a break with reality in the phenomenon of

[2] Consult Paul Tillich's penetrating analysis of the anxiety of guilt and
condemnation in *The Courage To Be* (New Haven: Yale University Press,
1952), pp. 51-54.

mental illness. Man's crying need is for reconciliation — reconciliation with God, with himself, and with his neighbor.

The basic problem is how man is to get back to God, for reconciliation with God is the key to self-acceptance and reconciliation with one's fellow man. Christian faith asserts that man can come to God only as God comes to man. The initiative is always on God's side. It is a matter of grace from beginning to end. Man in his sin can cut himself off from God but through his own efforts can never bring himself back to God. Every attempt to do so is an assertion of man's self-sufficiency, which is the very sin which has produced the alienation.

Fortunately, that which man needs but which he can never provide has been provided by God. The atonement is God's provision for the problem of estrangement created by human sin. The Bible bears witness to the redemptive activity of God in human history in the deliverance of Israel from bondage in Egypt, in the calling of Israel to be God's people and the vehicle of his revelation, in the judgment upon Israel for her sins and the narrowing of God's redemptive purpose to the remnant, the faithful within Israel. This redemptive activity of God in human history reaches its culmination in Jesus, the Son of God and Son of Man, the Messiah and Suffering Servant, who through his incarnation, life, death, and resurrection has opened up the way of eternal salvation for all mankind.

J. S. Whale writes with true insight:

> There are many religions which know no divine welcome to the sinner until he has ceased to be one. They would first make him righteous, and then bid him welcome to God. But God in Christ first welcomes him, and so makes him penitent and redeems him. The one demands newness of life; the other imparts it. The one demands human righteousness as the price of divine atonement; the other makes atonement in order to evoke righteousness. Christianity brings man to God by bringing God to man. The glory of the Gospel is the free pardon of God, offered to all who will receive it in humble faith.[3]

The saving activity of God in history in providing a way of salvation in Christ becomes effective for our salvation as it evokes faith, resulting in man's reconciliation to God. Rec-

[3] J. S. Whale, *Christian Doctrine* (Cambridge University Press, 1956), pp. 78-79.

onciliation to God in turn becomes the basis for self-acceptance, for man can now accept himself, knowing that he is accepted by God. Moreover, reconciliation with God is the basis for reconciliation with one's fellow man. In the light of the atonement in Christ one sees his neighbor as a brother for whom Christ died.

Summing up, we may say that the atonement is God's saving act. It is accomplished in history, and it is centered in his Son, Jesus Christ. Its effectiveness is conditioned by repentance and faith. When so accepted it issues in reconciliation — reconciliation to God, to one's self, and to one's fellow man.

Since the appearance of Anselm's epoch-making *Cur Deus Homo?* (1098), the doctrine of the atonement has ever been central in Christian theology. Upon the centrality of the doctrine theologians are generally agreed, but with regard to the interpretation of the atonement a great diversity of views has prevailed. In the history of Christian doctrine problems of Christology were met in controversy in the fourth and fifth centuries, and the Christological formulas of the Council of Nicea (325 A.D.) and the Council of Constantinople (381 A.D.) were further elaborated in the decree of the Council of Chalcedon (451 A.D.). This formulation of the Council of Chalcedon became recognized as the orthodox view of the person of Christ. Since it was never questioned by the reformers of the sixteenth century, it has been recognized as the orthodox view of all Christendom. However, in the sense that the Chalcedonian Christology is recognized as the orthodox view of the person of Christ, there never has been an orthodox view of the work of Christ, of the atonement.

As we attempt an interpretation of the atonement we are mindful that we are not embarking upon a voyage over an uncharted sea. Others before us have grappled with the problem. Thus before a constructive statement of the doctrine of the atonement can be made, it is necessary to set forth and evaluate the historical interpretations of the doctrine and the problems arising from them. But since the historical interpretations claim for themselves biblical support, a clear grasp of the relevant biblical materials is essential for an evaluation of the historical interpretations and the problems which they pose. Moreover, the biblical materials, both the Old Testament foundations and the New Testament witness, supply the basic categories for

any adequate constructive statement of the doctrine of the
atonement.

Thus the approach to be followed becomes clear:

Chapter One: The Old Testament Foundations of the Doctrine
of the Atonement.

Chapter Two: The New Testament Witness Concerning the
Atonement.

Chapter Three: Historical Interpretations of the Atonement.

Chapter Four: Special Problems.

Chapter Five: A Constructive Statement of the Doctrine of the
Atonement.

Chapter One

The Old Testament Foundations of the Doctrine of the Atonement

I. THE ELECTION OF ISRAEL AND THE COVENANT

The first foundation stone for the doctrine of the atonement is the Old Testament witness to Yahweh's choice of Israel as a nation to be his people and his entering into a covenant relation with her.

Yahweh redeems Israel from bondage in Egypt, and through this redemptive act he reveals his purpose: that he should be Israel's God and that Israel should be his people. This purpose is given contractual form in the covenant relationship. This is not to be interpreted as a contract between two equals, though the Hebrew word *b'rith* was sometimes used with this meaning (Gen. 21:27; I Sam. 18:3). The covenant is rooted in the divine sovereignty. It is based upon an act of redemption, which is an expression of pure grace. "You have seen what I did to the Egyptians, and how I bore you on eagles' wings and brought you to myself" (Ex. 19:4). It is Yahweh who imposes the conditions of the covenant and enunciates the blessings which will follow obedience. "Now therefore, if you will obey my voice and keep my covenant, you shall be my own possession among all the peoples; for all the earth is mine, and you shall be to me a kingdom of priests and a holy nation" (Ex. 19:5-6). It is Israel who accepts the conditions of the covenant as imposed by Yahweh: "All that the Lord has spoken we will do" (Ex. 19:8). This covenant relation is solemnized in the ritual acts of a sacrificial character described in Exodus 24:3-11. The ethical demands of Yahweh which the covenant relation imposes find expression in the Ten Commandments (Deut. 4:13).

The fundamental meaning of this biblical witness is that redemption is anchored in history. It is not based upon abstract ideas of God and salvation arrived at through processes of human logic. Rather it is based on the redemptive acts of God in the history of Israel, interpreted with the prophetic insight born of divine inspiration. This is what the theologians call "the scandal of particularity," a scandal which reaches its climax in the Christ-event.

The exodus from Egypt, the call of Israel, and the establishment of the covenant are the focal points of Old Testament history. This is the gospel, the *kerygma,* of the Old Testament. "As for election," writes John Bright, "we can find no period in Israel's history when she did not believe that she was the chosen people of Yahweh, and that her calling had been signaled in the exodus deliverance."[1] In cultic credos of the earliest period (Deut. 6:20-25; 26:5-10a) and in ancient poems (Ex. 15:1-18), the idea of Israel's election finds expression.[2] In the deuteronomic and prophetic literature Israel's election is heralded. "But the Lord has taken you, and brought you forth out of the iron furnace, out of Egypt, to be a people of his own possession, as at this day" (Deut. 4:20). "When Israel was a child, I loved him, and out of Egypt I called my son" (Hos. 11:1). "I am the Lord your God from the land of Egypt" (Hos. 13:4). "On the day when I chose Israel, I swore to the seed of the house of Jacob, making myself known to them in the land of Egypt. . ." (Ezek. 20:5). For Deutero-Isaiah faith in God's great redemptive act in bringing Israel out of Egypt becomes the basis of confidence that Yahweh will deliver Israel from the Babylonian exile (Isa. 43:14-19). Moreover, the psalms which recite the mighty acts of God, with the excep-

1 John Bright, *A History of Israel* (London: SCM Press, 1960), p. 132.
2 *Ibid.,* p. 133.

tion of Psalm 105, give the primacy to the deliverance from the land of Egypt (Psalms 68, 77, 114, 135, 136).

Bright[3] maintains that the concept of the covenant is as primitive as the concept of election. "There can scarcely be any doubt," he says, "that Israel's very existence was founded on the belief that her ancestors had at Sinai covenanted with Yahweh to be his people."[4] Again Bright declares:

> Belief in election and covenant thus rested in the recollection of historical events ultimately as handed down by those participating in them, who were the nucleus of Israel. . . . As memory of these events was brought to Palestine by the group experiencing them, and as the amphictyony was formed about Yahwistic faith, exodus and Sinai became the normative tradition of all Israel: the ancestors of all of us were led by Yahweh through the sea and at Sinai in solemn covenant became his people.[5]

Walther Eichrodt regards the covenant relation as of such fundamental importance that in his great pioneer three-volume work on Old Testament theology, *Theologie des Alten Testaments,* he makes the covenant idea the basic framework for the treatment of the whole sweep of Old Testament theology. Other competent Old Testament scholars like H. Wheeler Robinson, H. H. Rowley, and G. Ernest Wright, while showing appreciation for Eichrodt's work, regard the idea of election as being more fundamental. But these two, election and the covenant, are not to be pulled apart, because they belong together. To borrow a phrase from Norman Snaith, it is the *ahabah,* the election-love, of Yahweh which establishes the covenant without any regard to merit on the part of Israel. And it is the *chesed,* the covenant-love, of Yahweh which sustains the covenant, despite the unfaithfulness of Israel.[6]

Though it is the exodus and the choice of Israel to be God's covenant people which is decisive for Israel's faith, the Old Testament represents this as going back to a prior choice, the choice of the patriarchs. The JE narratives of the Pentateuch emphasize God's choice of the patriarchs, particularly Abram

3 *Loc. cit.*
4 *Loc. cit.*
5 *Ibid.,* p. 134.
6 Norman Snaith, *The Distinctive Ideas of the Old Testament* (Philadelphia: Westminster Press, 1946).

(Gen. 12:1-3). H. Wheeler Robinson treats the choice of Abraham as an illustration of the principle of corporate personality.
He says: "The nation is not only represented by, but summed
up in, its ancestors. To call Abraham is to call the race that
springs from him."[7] In Deuteronomy the choice of Israel is
clearly represented as based on no merit on the part of Israel,
but as grounded in the *ahabah,* the election-love, of Yahweh.
Nevertheless, in thus choosing Israel Yahweh was keeping the
promise which he made to the patriarchs (Deut. 4:37; 7:6-8;
9:5, 27; 10:15). Robinson[8] asserts that the prophets are silent
as to an election of the patriarchs, but surely there is at least a
strong hint of this in the words: "But, you Israel, my servant,
Jacob, whom I have chosen, the offspring of Abraham, my
friend" (Isa. 41:8). The covenant with Abraham is clearly set
forth in the P narrative of the Pentateuch, and circumcision is
given as the sign of the covenant (Gen. 17). The covenant
promises made to Abraham were confirmed in promises to Isaac
and Jacob (Gen. 26:1-5; 28:10-17). Psalm 105 is a hymn of
praise to Yahweh for his countless blessings upon Israel from
the covenant with Abraham to the conquest of the land of
Canaan. The psalmist treats this whole period of history as a
single unit, making specific reference to the covenant with
Abraham, which was confirmed to Isaac and Jacob (verses 9,
10). The P material of the Pentateuch also speaks of a covenant with Noah, the sign of which is the rainbow (Gen. 9:
1-17). The significance of this covenant is in its universality,
a covenant "between me and you and every living creature
that is with you, for all future generations" (Gen. 9:12).

The Israelites were constantly tempted to misinterpret the
covenant relationship as carrying a guarantee of divine favor,
regardless of Israel's unfaithfulness. Against such distortions
of the covenant idea the prophets constantly inveighed. "You
only have I known of all the families of the earth; therefore I
will punish you for all your iniquities" (Amos 3:2). The
prophets warned that Israel would not escape the judgment of
Yahweh, the Day of the Lord. Rather the judgment upon Israel
would be particularly severe.

It is to be noted that the ideas of election and covenant,

---

[7] H. Wheeler Robinson, *Inspiration and Revelation in the Old Testament*
(Oxford University Press, 1953), p. 151.

[8] *Loc. cit.*

which seem to be exclusionistic ideas, really carry the seed of universalism. God's concern is not for Abraham alone, nor for Israel alone, but for all mankind. Election is for service. Special privilege carries with it special responsibility. God's purpose embraces all mankind. God's promise to Abram is that through him all the families of the earth will be blessed (Gen. 12:3). Israel is given the commission to be "a kingdom of priests and a holy nation" (Ex. 19:6). God's servant, Israel, is to be "a light to the nations" (Isa. 42:6; 49:6). To Israel is given the revelation of Yahweh as the one and only God. This God calls, "Turn to me and be saved, all the ends of the earth! For I am God, and there is no other" (Isa. 45:22).

God works in human history through a covenant people. The covenant is based upon a divine act of redemption. In the Old Testament the nation Israel is the covenant people, and the act of redemption is the deliverance from Egypt. In the New Testament the covenant people is the church, and the divine act of redemption upon which the covenant is based is redemption from sin through the atoning death of Christ.

II. Sacrifice as a Means of Atonement

The universality of sacrifice in the ancient world and the various theories regarding the origin of sacrifice, such as the gift theory (E. B. Tylor, Buchanan Gray), the communion theory (J. G. Frazer, W. Robertson Smith), and the life theory (E. O. James, F. C. N. Hicks, Vincent Taylor) need not concern us here. What is of most importance for our purpose is the meaning of sacrifice in the Old Testament, particularly in the priestly legislation, and the relation of this to the concepts of the covenant and the atonement for sin.

In a discussion as brief as this one must be, it is difficult to do justice to the complexity of the subject and to avoid the distortion which comes from oversimplification. Nevertheless, an attempt must be made, because an understanding of the meaning of sacrifice in the Old Testament is essential to the interpretation of much of the New Testament material related to the atonement, to an evaluation of many of the historical views of the atonement, and to a constructive interpretation of the meaning of the death of Christ.

Through the work of the prophets a deepened understanding of the meaning of sin was given to Israel. All sin was sin

against Yahweh, the covenant God. It was Israel's breach of
the covenant. Within the context of this understanding of sin
arose the idea of atoning sacrifices as a manifestation of the
grace of Yahweh. It was Yahweh's appointed way of removing
the sin barrier, of restoring the covenant, of bringing Israel back
into fellowship with the covenant God. Atoning sacrifices, then,
were not so much man's gift to God as God's gift to man. "For
the life of the flesh is in the blood; and I have given it for you
upon the altar to make atonement for your souls . . ." (Lev.
17:11). Here it is stated that the blood through which the
atonement is effected is a gift from Yahweh. Basic to an understanding of the priestly legislation of the Old Testament is the
conviction that the provision for sacrificial worship is made by
the covenant God himself. Walther Eichrodt says: "The appara-
tus of sacrifice is itself a gift graciously vouchsafed by the covenant God in order to give man the opportunity for confession
and reparation."[9]

One of the main difficulties in the attempt to interpret the
meaning of sacrifice in the Old Testament is the fact that,
despite the abundance of the references to sacrifice and the mi-
nuteness of the descriptions of the ritual of sacrifice, the Old
Testament itself makes no attempt to give a rationale of sacrifice. Thus an attempt to explain what sacrifice meant to the
Hebrews involves the necessity of drawing inferences from what
are at best only hints in the Old Testament material. Moreover,
because of the difficulties involved in trying to get an adequate
understanding of sacrifice by such a method, the temptation
is strong to try to explain the meaning of sacrifice in the Old
Testament on the basis of the analogy of the meaning of sacrifice in other religions of the ancient world. However, such a
process should be avoided as much as possible because of the
danger of ignoring the uniqueness of Israel's religion and of
reading into it ideas fundamentally alien to it.

Though dogmatism is not in order, it seems safe to say that
it is easier to point out errors in prevailing views than it is to
supply a constructive interpretation. The most common mis-
interpretation of sacrifice in the Old Testament is that which is
associated with the view of penal substitution. With regard to
atoning sacrifices in the Old Testament, this is the view which

9 Walther Eichrodt, *The Theology of the Old Testament* (Philadelphia:
Westminster Press, 1961), Vol. I, p. 164.

assumes that there is a transfer of guilt from the worshipper to the sacrificial victim, that the innocent animal is punished in the place of the worshipper, and that the worshipper is thus delivered from the punishment which he deserves because of his sin.

Advocates of the penal substitution view usually base their interpretations on the following three premises: that in the ritual of sacrifice the worshipper in placing his hands upon the head of the sacrificial victim thereby signifies the transference of guilt from himself to the innocent animal, that in sacrifice the blood signified death not life, and that sacrifice is to be interpreted in terms of propitiation, the primary purpose being that of appeasing the wrath of an angry deity. It is the contention of this writer that all three of these premises are wrong.

That the worshipper's laying his hands upon the head of the sacrificial victim in the ritual of sacrifice (Lev. 1:4; 3:2; 4:4) does not signify the transference of guilt seems fairly certain. If a transfer of guilt were involved, the victim would then be regarded as unclean. But as a matter of fact it is always treated as especially holy. The idea of the transference of guilt is doubtless based upon the part of the ritual of the Day of Atonement described in Leviticus 16:21:

> And Aaron shall lay both his hands upon the head of the live goat, and confess over him all the iniquities of the people of Israel, and all their transgressions, all their sins; and he shall put them upon the head of the goat, and send him away into the wilderness by the hand of a man who is in readiness.

Here the idea of the transference of guilt is clearly expressed. "The goat shall bear all their iniquities upon him to a solitary land" (Lev. 16:22). However, what is of decisive importance is that the goat was not a sacrifice to Yahweh; but it was led away into the wilderness for Azazel, which, according to one interpretation, was a demon regarded as residing in the desert. "In admitting that sins could be put upon the head of an animal and borne away into the wilderness, they confessed the inadequacy of the existing system."[10] The fact of the matter is that the atoning sacrifices prescribed by the Old Testament were designed to cover ritualistic sins, or sins of inadvertence, but they were regarded as

[10] Vincent Taylor, *Jesus and His Sacrifice* (London: Macmillan and Company, 1948), p. 56.

having no efficacy for sins done with a high hand. For these the sinner
had to bear his own iniquity (Num. 15:27-31). The only exception to
this was the ritual of the scapegoat on the Day of Atonement; but, as
we have noted, this was not a sacrifice at all. The statement, "The goat
shall bear all their inquities upon him to a solitary land" (Lev. 16:22), is
not to be interpreted in terms of penal substitution. "The idea is not
that the goat was suffering the sufferings that were due to sinners, but
that it was carrying away their sins."[11]

What the worshipper's laying his hands upon the head of the
victim in the ritual of sacrifice did mean is not so easy to determine. The clearest hint as to the meaning which the Bible
gives is found in the words, "And it shall be accepted for him
to make atonement for him" (Lev. 1:4). Eichrodt interprets
the laying on of hands in the ritual of sacrifice to mean that the
worshipper identifies the sacrificial victim as belonging to himself and expresses his willingness to surrender it.[12] This much
it seems safe to say. Probably one can go a step further, however, and say that in this ritual act the worshipper identifies
himself with the sacrificial victim, so that thereafter what happens to the sacrificial victim, at least symbolically, happens to
the worshipper himself.[13]

With regard to the second premise, it seems that in the use
of blood in the ritual of sacrifice the emphasis is placed upon
life, not death. Those who favor the emphasis upon death
usually point out that in the use of the Hebrew word for blood,
dam, the majority of Old Testament references are to some kind
of violent death.[14] However, it must be remembered that these
references to blood in relation to violent death (e.g., Gen. 9:6;
Num. 35:19) have no connection with the blood of sacrificial
worship. Moreover, the crucial passage in the Old Testament,
that which comes closer to giving a rationale of sacrifice than any
other, specifically interprets the meaning of blood in terms of
life. "For the life of the flesh is in the blood; and I have given
it for you upon the altar to make atonement for your souls; for

11 C. Ryder Smith, *The Bible Doctrine of Salvation* (London: The Epworth Press, revised edition, 1946) , p. 80.

12 Eichrodt, *op. cit.*, pp. 165-66.

13 So F.C.N. Hicks, C. Ryder Smith, Vincent Taylor.

14 Cf. Leon Morris, *The Apostolic Preaching of the Cross* (London:
The Tyndale Press, 1955) , pp. 108-110.

it is the blood that makes atonement, by reason of the life" (Lev. 17:11; cf. Gen. 9:4-5; Deut. 12:23; Lev. 3:17; 7:26f.; 17:10, 12, 14; II Sam. 23:17; Psa. 72:14).

Eichrodt[15] lists three other arguments against the substitutionary interpretation of the death of the animal slaughtered in sacrifice, and all three are related to the meaning of blood. First, if the principal action were the slaying of the victim as the execution of the death penalty, it ought to be done by the priest rather than by the worshipper as the priestly law prescribes. The fact of the matter is, however, that the emphasis is placed upon the manipulation of the blood by the priest, the idea being, particularly on the Day of Atonement, of taking the blood as near as possible to the deity. Second, the fact that in the case of a very poor person an offering of fine flour would suffice for the sin offering (Lev. 5:11-13), an offering in which no death took place and no blood was shed, is an argument against the interpretation of penal substitution. Third, "The offences atoned for by the sacrifice are, at any rate in the present text of the Priestly Code, none of them sins worthy of death."[16]

Hearty approval should be given to the statement by Smith:

> No doubt all the ritual, including the offering of the animals, was practiced 'on behalf of' or for the benefit of the worshippers, but there is no hint, either on the Day of Atonement or elsewhere, of the idea that a victim suffered the sufferings that a worshipper ought to have suffered, or was punished with the punishment that was his due, or died the death that he ought to have died.[17]

The third mistaken premise is that the Old Testament sacrifices were basically propitiatory in character, designed to appease the wrath of God. To say that this is a mistaken premise is not to deny the concept of the wrath of God, nor to indicate that God is indifferent to human sin. But this is to say that the wrath of God is not analogous to the wrath of man, and that the Hebrew idea of sacrifice is not analogous to the crude pagan ideas in which the angry deity is bought off and his wrath appeased by the blood of the sacrificial victim.

15 Op. cit., p. 165.
16 Loc. cit.
17 Op. cit., p. 79.

The Hebrew term translated "to make atonement" is *kipper*. Concerning the usage of this term Taylor says:

> In cases where it means 'to appease' or 'pacify' the reference is to man. In other passages it is used of expiation for sin apart from sacrifice, and where God is the subject the meaning is 'to forgive' or 'to purge away.' The commonest use of the verb is in connection with sacrificial rites, and here the thought is that of covering ritual imperfections or of expiating sins.[18]

It is the work of C. H. Dodd,[19] perhaps more than that of anyone else, which has led to the wide acceptance of these conclusions. On the basis of a very technical study of the terms used in the Septuagint to translate *kipper* he concludes that the translators of the Septuagint did not regard *kipper* (when used as a religious term) as "conveying the sense of propitiating the Deity" but understood it in the sense of "performing an act whereby guilt or defilement is removed."[20]

> Thus Hellenistic Judaism, as represented by the LXX, does not regard the cultus as a means of pacifying the displeasure of the Deity, but as a means of delivering man from sin, and it looks in the last resort to God himself to perform that deliverance. . . . [21]

The fact that it is God himself who covers the sin is the basic difference in the understanding of sacrifice manifested in the Old Testament as compared with that in heathen religions. It is God himself who manifests his grace to man in providing a means of covering sin so that it no longer has the power of disturbing the covenant relation between God and man.[22]

Here we are approaching a positive statement of the meaning of sacrifice. Sacrifice offered a means for the sinner to make his approach to the righteous and holy God. Sacrifice was a means of dramatizing the sinner's repentance, of covering his sin, and of providing a means of self-surrender to God.

> No Hebrew could think of offering himself as he was, frail and sinful to a holy and righteous God, while the idea of a

[18] Taylor, *op. cit.*, p. 52.
[19] Cf. *The Bible and the Greeks* (London: Hodder & Stoughton, second impression, 1954), pp. 82-95.
[20] *Ibid.*, p. 93.
[21] *Loc. cit.*
[22] P. T. Forsyth, *The Work of Christ* (London: Hodder & Stoughton), p. 55.

purely spiritual offering would have seemed to him abstract and meaningless. The life offered must be that of another, innocent and pure, free from all impurity and sin, and yet withal the symbol of the ideal life to which he aspired and with which he could identify himself.[23]

The fact that "sin is not forgiven as a matter of course, but as the result of the offering of a pure and innocent life as expiation for the guilt-laden life of the offerer" conveys "a deep and impressive lesson on the seriousness of sin."[24]

The passive character of the sacrificial victim, the fact that sacrifices were efficacious only for inadvertent sins or ritual sins, leaving untouched the most serious sins, and the liability to abuse, the forgiveness of sins being interpreted as the automatic result of the correct performance of the ritual — all of these were serious defects which made sacrificial worship at its best of only limited value as a means of approach to God. The severe criticism of sacrificial worship by the prophets, sounding at times like an almost complete repudiation of the sacrificial system (e.g., Amos 5:21-26; Isa. 1:11; Micah 6:7-8; Jer. 7:22), is not to be regarded as a rejection of sacrificial worship as such. Rather it is to be interpreted to mean that ritual is no substitute for righteousness, that sacrifice is not to be a substitute for repentance and dedication but a vehicle of their expression.[25] For example, the attitude of Isaiah toward the people's prayers (Isa. 1:15) is just as negative as his attitude toward their sacrifices (Isa. 1:11), but surely one is not to say on the basis of this that Isaiah is repudiating prayer as such. The main concern of the prophets was that the weighty requirements of God such as justice, mercy, and an humble walk with God (Hos. 12:6; Micah 6:8) should not be neglected in an undue emphasis upon sacrifice.

The psalms express a variety of attitudes toward sacrificial worship, ranging from warm appreciation (Psa. 51:19;54:6; 66:13-15) to severe criticism (Psa. 40:6; 51:16). And the critical notes are sounded in a constructive manner as if to say, "Not that but this, not formalistic worship, but a humble worship from the heart!" "The sacrifice acceptable to God is a broken

23 Taylor, *op. cit.*, p. 60.
24 Eichrodt, *op. cit.*, p. 166.
25 Cf. F. C. N. Hicks, *The Fullness of Sacrifice* (London: Macmillan and Company, 1930), pp. 55-91.

spirit; a broken and contrite heart, O God, thou wilt not despise" (Psa. 51:17). "Offer to God a sacrifice of thanksgiving . . . ." "He who brings thanksgiving as his sacrifice honors me" (Psa. 50:14, 23; cf. 107:22; 116:17).

> Sacrifice and offering thou dost not desire; but thou hast given me an open ear. Burnt offering and sin offering thou hast not required. Then I said, "Lo, I come; in the roll of the book it is written of me; I delight to do thy will, O my God; thy law is within my heart" (Psa. 40:6-8).

An ear attentive to the Lord's voice, a heart that delights to do his will! In this is the spiritual meaning of sacrifice. And upon this the New Testament builds (Rom. 12:1-2; Heb. 10:5-10).

III. THE MESSIANIC KING

The expectation of a messianic king in the Old Testament is a part of a much larger hope, the messianic hope. This was Israel's indomitable expectation of a glorious future, and it was "about synonymous with the eschatology of the nation."[26] Since a discussion of the messianic hope as such would take us far afield of our purpose, our attention will be confined to the hope of the coming of a messianic king.

For a proper evaluation of this hope attention must be centered upon the origin and development of the monarchy in the experience of Israel. The Old Testament sources reveal the existence of an ambivalent attitude towards Israel's having a king. On the one hand, the attitude is expressed that the demand for a king is a rejection of the sovereignty of Yahweh (Judges 8:23; I Sam. 8:4-9; 12:17), and that only a person of inferior quality, a mere bramble bush of a man would want to be king (Judges 9:7-21). On the other hand, the attitude is also strongly expressed that Israel's acceptance of a king involves no rejection of Yahweh's sovereignty, but that the king is the agent through whom this sovereignty will be realized (I Sam. 10:17-27a; Psa. 2; 18; 20; 21; 45; 72; 89; 101; 110; 132; 144:1-11). Though for the most part these two attitudes were held by two different groups of people, Samuel is represented as having entertained them both.

Fundamentally, the problem was that of the tension between

---

[26] A. C. Knudson, *The Religious Teaching of the Old Testament* (New York: Abingdon Cokesbury Press, 1918), p. 351.

the ideal of charismatic leadership and dynastic leadership. The early leaders of Israel had all been charismatic leaders, whose natural abilities and endowment with the Spirit of Yahweh had fitted them for their leadership responsibilities. In keeping with this ideal, the first two kings of Israel, Saul and David, were both charismatic leaders. The fact that Israel's second king was not a son of Saul — despite the abortive attempt to establish one of Saul's sons on the throne — was probably due to the fact that the charismatic qualities that Saul had displayed before becoming king and in the early years of his reign were no longer in evidence during the latter years of his reign, and to the obvious fact that Yahweh had chosen David to be king and endowed him with the qualities of leadership necessary for the successful execution of his responsibilities. Moreover, David's outstanding success as a military leader in driving out the enemies of Israel and in extending the limits of Israel's dominion, his sagacity in politics, and his spiritual leadership established the kingdom so firmly in David's hands that "by the time David grew old, the question was not *if* his son would succeed him, but only *which* son would do so. . . ."[27] The tradition even arose that God had made an eternal covenant with David, promising to establish a son of David upon the throne of Israel forever (II Sam. 23:5; 7:11-16). The principle of dynastic rule had replaced that of charismatic leadership.

By making Jerusalem his capital and calling it "the city of David," by bringing the ark to Jerusalem and initiating plans to build a magnificent temple for Yahweh — these plans being carried out by David's son, Solomon — David had dramatized the principle of the king as the agent of Yahweh. However, in doing so he had effected a union between church and state, which, by closely allying religion with the Davidic dynasty, was always in danger of hallowing the political policies of the monarchy in the name of religion.

It was probably this close union of church and state in the figure of the Davidic king which brought forth the enthronement psalms (47, 93-99) and the royal psalms (2, 18, 20, 21, 45, 72, 89, 101, 110, 132, 144:1-11). The so-called enthronement psalms emphasize the sovereignty of Yahweh and are characterized by the words, *Yhwh malak,* which should probably be translated,

---

[27] John Bright, *The Kingdom of God* (New York: Abingdon Press, 1953), p. 40.

" 'It is Yahweh who reigns' or the like, rather than 'Yahweh has become king.' "[28] The so-called royal psalms praise the glories of the Davidic king, representing him as God's son (Psa. 2:7) and the agent of his reign.[29]

Year by year as the glories of the Davidic king were celebrated in the cult, the disparity between the ideal and the existing situation became apparent. This gave rise to the hope that in the future the ideal king of the Davidic line would come. The people in times of hardship and oppression began to look back to the Davidic era with a feeling of nostalgia. David's imperfections tended to be forgotten and his glories magnified. The golden age in the past under David would be surpassed by an even greater golden age in the future under "great David's greater son."

Though in many passages which speak of the golden age in the future no mention at all is made of the Davidic king and Yahweh himself is the agent of deliverance (e.g., Isa. 40), and though in some passages the Davidic king comes on the scene only after Yahweh has restored the fortunes of his people (e.g., Ezek. 34), and though in some passages the concept of the ideal kingship is divorced from the Davidic dynasty (e.g., Hag. 2:23; Zech. 3:8; 6:12), nevertheless, the concept of the ideal Davidic king emerges as one of the most important facets of the messianic hope. Epithets of a semi-divine nature (Isa. 9:6-7) are applied to the Davidic king. The Spirit of Yahweh rests upon him, and he rules with justice and equity (Isa. 11:1-5; cf. 16:5) and ushers in a new era of peace (Isa. 11:6-9; Micah 5:2-5; Zech. 9:1-10).[30] The name by which he is called, "The Lord is our righteousness," (Jer. 23:5-6; 33:14-17) emphasizes the fact that he is Yahweh's agent. In short, there emerges a composite portrait of an ideal Davidic king who will throw off the yoke of Israel's oppressors, restore to the nation its ancient glories, and inaugurate a benevolent reign of righteousness and peace.[31]

The term "Messiah" is a transliteration of the Hebrew *mashiach*. Its literal meaning is "anointed" or "anointed one." Typically it is used of Israel's kings (e.g., I Sam. 24:6; II Sam.

28 Bright, *A History of Israel*, p. 206.

29 The complicated problem of the New Year's festival in the Near East and its relation to this problem cannot be dealt with here.

30 The passage in Zechariah, however, does not specifically connect the king with David.

31 Taylor, *op. cit.*, pp. 16-17.

22:51), but it is also applied to priests (Lev. 4:5; 6:22) ; and the verb form is used in reference to prophets, sometimes in a literal and sometimes in a spiritual sense (I Kings 19:15-16; Isa. 61:1). Even the heathen king Cyrus is designated as Yahweh's anointed in the sense that Yahweh has selected him to achieve his purpose (Isa. 45:1). There is also an enigmatic use of the term, probably as a title, in Daniel 9:25.

Davidson suggests that the title "Messiah" as applied to a future king of prophetic and popular expectation is derived from Psalm 2:2: "The kings of the earth set themselves, and the rulers take counsel together, against the Lord and against his anointed."[32] On the other hand, Dalman suggests that Messiah in its later sense is a shortened form of "Jhwh's Anointed" and that no single passage of the Old Testament was responsible for its adoption.[33] At any rate, it seems safe to say that by the time of Jesus "Messiah" was the term which suggested to the average Jew the hope of the ideal king of the Davidic line, the one who would deliver Israel from political oppression and establish a reign of righteousness and peace (Luke 1:67-79; Mark 12:35; 8:29-33; John 1:20, 25; 3:28; 6:15; 7:27, 31, 41b, 42; 9:22; 12:34).

The basic problem is the sovereignty of God in human history and how this sovereignty is to be established. One Old Testament answer to this problem is that it is to be established through the activity of a messianic king of the Davidic line. As the New Testament witnesses, Jesus came forth proclaiming the kingdom of God and asserting that the sovereignty of God in human history was being established through him. But as we shall see in our study of the New Testament witness he regarded himself as a spiritual king, not a political ruler. He believed the sovereignty of God would be realized through the fulfilment of the role of the Suffering Servant, not that of the military conqueror of the Davidic line.

IV. THE SERVANT OF YAHWEH

Ever since B. Duhm in 1875 published his *Die Theologie der Propheten,* isolating four Servant Songs from the text of Isaiah 40-55 (Isa. 42:1-7; 49:1-6; 50:4-9; 52:13-53:12), it has been the

---

[32] A. B. Davidson, *Old Testament Prophecy* (Edinburgh: T. & T. Clark, 1905), p. 309.

[33] Dalman, *The Words of Jesus,* p. 291, cited by C. W. Emmet, "Messiah," *Encyclopaedia of Religion and Ethics,* James Hastings, editor (Edinburgh: T. & T. Clark, 1915), Vol. 8, p. 571.

custom among Old Testament scholars to speak of the Servant Songs in Deutero-Isaiah. Though some scholars have objected to the separation of these passages from the main body of the prophecy, and though there has not been complete unanimity concerning the exact limits of the songs[34] or concerning their number, nevertheless, the great majority of Old Testament scholars have followed Duhm to such an extent that "the existence of the four Servant Songs has come to be regarded as one of the firm results of modern O.T. study."[35]

Probably no problem in the Old Testament field has occupied the scholars so much as that of the identification of the Servant. The literature in this field is so voluminous that even a brief summary of the basic positions would entail an inordinately lengthy digression.[36] Some of the leading answers which have been proposed are that the Servant in the Songs is Israel, ideal Israel, the remnant, a mythological figure, the Messiah, or an historical figure such as Moses, Hezekiah, Jehoiachin, Jeremiah, Ezekiel, Cyrus, Zerubbabel, Deutero-Isaiah himself, or a combination of several of these.

The position taken here, briefly stated, is that in the Servant Songs the concept of the Servant is a fluid one, capable of contraction or expansion. This is in accord with the Old Testament idea of corporate personality by which the group may represent the individual or the individual the group. In the first song the Servant is Israel, as is clearly the case in the uses of the term in Deutero-Isaiah outside the songs (Isa. 41:8; 44:1, 21; 45:4; 48:20). In the second song, though the Servant is specifically designated as Israel (Isa. 49:3), the concept seems to narrow to the faithful within Israel, because the Servant has a mission to Israel (49: 5-6). In the third song there is a further individualizing of the details of the portrait, while in the fourth song the details are so individualistic that a purely corporate interpretation can be maintained only with the greatest difficulty. And yet the

34 Duhm himself in a commentary published in 1892 changed the limits of the first song to Isa. 42:1-4.

35 Norman H. Snaith, "The Servant of the Lord in Deutero-Isaiah," *Studies in Old Testament Prophecy*, H. H. Rowley, editor (Edinburgh: T. & T. Clark, 1950), p. 187.

36 For a comprehensive summary of the critical interpretations consult Christopher R. North, *The Suffering Servant in Deutero-Isaiah* (London: Oxford University Press, 1950). Cf. also H. H. Rowley, *The Servant of the Lord and Other Essays on the Old Testament* (London: Lutterworth Press, 1952).

very fluidity of the conception makes it possible to maintain that the corporate concept is never entirely abandoned. But regardless of what conception of the Servant the prophet himself entertained, the Suffering Servant ideal finds its expression and most complete fulfilment in Jesus and his church.

The first song (Isa. 42:1-4) describes the mission of the Servant as that of bringing forth justice to the nations, of establishing justice in the earth; and it delineates the Servant's qualifications for his work. The mission of the Servant in the second song (Isa. 49:1-6) is that of gathering Israel to Yahweh and of being a light to the nations (Isa. 49:1-6). In the third song (Isa. 50:4-9) it is indicated that the Servant's mission will involve him in suffering, but that he will be faithful because he anticipates vindication by Yahweh. In the fourth song (Isa. 52:13-53:12) the mission of the Servant is interpreted as that of sin-bearing, and the suffering of the Servant is interpreted as vicarious. It is not incidental to the Servant's mission, but is the indispensable means by which the mission is discharged.

Our main concern in this study is with the concept of redemption from sin through vicarious suffering voluntarily accepted, as set forth in the fourth Servant poem. Here Old Testament thought reaches its apex in a new and startling conception almost ignored in the rest of the Old Testament[37] but destined to become the keystone of New Testament faith.

It is possible that Moses' intercession for his people (Ex. 32:30-34) and Jeremiah's identification with sinful Judah (e.g., Jer. 8:21-9:1) may have supplied the unknown author of this song with types for his conception, but the grandeur of the Servant conception far exceeds that of any of the prototypes. The Servant is completely innocent, he suffers in silence, he is slain, and is raised from the dead (53:6-12). None of these things can be said of Moses or Jeremiah. Israel's experience in the exile was probably also in the background of the prophet's conception. It may have been the exile and the anticipated restoration which suggested the idea of death and resurrection.

The fourth Servant song is divided into five stanzas of three verses each. Christopher North suggests the themes of the five stanzas as follows:

> the future exaltation of the Servant (52:13-15), man of sorrows (53:1-3), his vicarious sufferings (53:4-6), his ignominious death

---

[37] There are possibly echoes of this idea in Psa. 22; Zech. 9:9-10; 12:9-14.

(53:7-9), his resurrection and reward (53:10-12). Yahweh is
the speaker in the beginning and end of the song (52:13-15;
53:11-12), but the speakers in the central part of the song are
penitent peoples, probably Jews and Gentiles, who are con-
fessing the impression made upon them by the sufferings of the
Servant (53:1-10).[38]

The changing attitude of the onlookers towards the Servant's
suffering is the theme of 53:1-6.

> At first they were bewildered by the Servant's suffering; then
> they thought it contemptible, thus passing upon it an intel-
> lectual judgment; then, forced to seek a moral reason for it,
> they accounted it as penal and due to the Servant for his own
> sin; then they recognized that its penalty was vicarious, and the
> Servant was suffering for them; and finally they knew that it was
> redemptive, the means of their own healing and peace.[39]

Five characteristics of the sufferings of the Servant are to be
noted. The first is the innocence of the Servant and the silence
and the voluntariness of the suffering. In the exile Israel had
suffered for her sin. But the Servant's suffering was innocent.
"He had done no violence, and there was no deceit in his mouth"
(53:9). He is Yahweh's righteous Servant (53:11). He was
silent like a lamb led to the slaughter or a sheep before its
shearers (53:7). He made himself an offering for sin (53:10).

The second characteristic of his sufferings was their complete-
ness. "He was despised and rejected of men; a man of sorrows,
and acquainted with grief" (53:3). He was wounded, bruised
and chastised (53:5), oppressed and afflicted (53:7). "He poured
out his soul to death, and was numbered with the transgressors"
(53:12). "He was cut off out of the land of the living" (53:8),
and he was buried with the wicked (53:9).

The will of Yahweh in connection with the sufferings of the
Servant is the third thing which calls for emphasis. The sufferings of the Servant are not by chance. There was a divine
purpose behind them. "The Lord has laid on him the iniquity
of us all" (53:6). "Yet it was the will of the Lord to bruise
him; he has put him to grief" (53:10). "The will of the Lord
shall prosper in his hand" (53:10).

38 Christopher North, *Isaiah 40-55: Introduction and Commentary* (London: SCM Press, 1952), pp. 131-38.

39 George Adam Smith, "The Book of Isaiah," *The Expositor's Bible*
(Grand Rapids: Wm. B. Eerdmans Publishing Co., 1947), Vol. III, pp. 817-18.

In the fourth place the sufferings of the Servant are vicarious in nature and redemptive in effect. Vicariousness is indicated by such words as these: "Surely he has borne our griefs and carried our sorrows. . . . But he was wounded for our transgressions, he was bruised for our iniquities" (53:4-5). "The Lord has laid on him the iniquity of us all" (53:6). He was "stricken for the transgression of my people" (53:8). "He bore the sin of many, and made intercession for the transgressors" (53:12). The Servant's sufferings were redemptive in their effect. They brought peace, healing, righteousness, and a new relation to God (53:5, 10, 11). The sufferings are redemptive in effect because they express God's judgment on sin and evoke a response of penitent confession. The sufferings of the Servant are described as a guilt offering (*asham*, 53:10).[40] The Old Testament law of the guilt offering required that restitution be made, adding one fifth. This was prior to the offering of the guilt offering (Lev. 5:14-6:7). The fact that restitution was followed by the guilt offering seems to imply that ultimately the sin was against God and that God himself, through the means of sacrifice which he has provided, has to remove the sin barrier and open up the way for restored fellowship. Moreover, as Taylor indicates, "It is the complete act, including the Servant's offering and the onlooker's response, which constitutes the sacrifice presented to God."[41] According to Fosdick, it is the concept of "corporate personality" whereby "the sin of one could be the curse of all" which supplies the basis for the great Isaiah's announcement of a sacrifice of one — the Suffering Servant — which could be "the redemption of all."[42]

Finally, the victory of the Servant should be emphasized. Excruciating pain and an ignominious death are followed by a victorious resurrection (53:10-12). "After the suffering had been fulfilled the triumph had come. The Servant divided the spoil with the strong; and his spoil was men won to God, forgiven, healed, made righteous."[43] The offspring which he sees, the fruit of the travail of his soul which brings him satisfaction

[40] Cf. H. Wheeler Robinson's interpretation, *The Cross of the Servant* (Philadelphia: Westminster Press, 1955), p. 87.

[41] Taylor, *op. cit.*, p. 42.

[42] Harry Emerson Fosdick, *A Guide to Understanding the Bible* (New York: Harper and Row, 1938, sixteenth edition), p. 175.

[43] Fleming James, *Personalities of the Old Testament* (New York: Charles Scribner's Sons, 1947), pp. 386-87.

(53:10, 11), is "the vast throng of the redeemed."[44] Through his suffering the Servant fulfills his mission. He establishes justice in the earth (Isa. 42:4); he restores Israel to God; and he becomes a light to the Gentiles (49:5-6).

In Isaiah 53 there is a harmonious blending of the categories of sacrifice and vicarious suffering. The references to sin-bearing suggest the scapegoat of the ritual on the Day of Atonement (Lev. 16:20-23). We have already taken note of the fact that, though the ritual of the scapegoat is set forth in a context of sacrifice, the goat itself was not a sacrificial victim. The lamb of 53:7 may be a sacrificial victim, though this is not necessarily the case (cf. Jer. 11:19). The clearest reference to the ritual of sacrifice, however, is in the mention of the guilt offering in verse 10. But in Isaiah 53 the meaning of sacrifice is transmuted. In the ritual of sacrifice no attention is focused upon the suffering of the victim, but in the fourth Servant Song the suffering of the Servant receives primary emphasis. It is one of the chief factors which evoke the response of penitent confession, another big factor being the Servant's exaltation by Yahweh (Isa. 52:13-15; 53:10-12). In the ritual of sacrifice the victim is an animal whose innocence and purity are nonmoral, but in Isaiah 53 the victim is a person whose innocence and purity are moral and spiritual. The idea of sacrifice is thus spiritualized. The priest and the victim are one. The sacrifice of the Servant is his complete obedience to the will of Yahweh, his entering into "the consequences of God's judgment on sin,"[45] the voluntary self-giving of love for the redemption of sinners. Such a sacrifice, when accepted by those for whom it is made in penitence and faith, is effective for restoring man's broken fellowship with God, bringing healing, peace, and righteousness.

The Old Testament ideal of the Suffering Servant shows us that sin can be expiated only as it is borne in vicarious suffering. The Old Testament itself, however, provides no fulfilment of the Suffering Servant ideal. But as we shall see in our study of the New Testament witness Jesus interpreted his mission as that of the fulfilment of the Suffering Servant ideal, and it is this ideal which supplies a basic category for the interpretation of the atonement.

---

44 Loc. cit.

45 William J. Wolf, No Cross, No Crown (Garden City: Doubleday & Company, 1957), p. 36.

Chapter Two

The New Testament Witness Concerning the Atonement

I. THE UNITY OF SALVATION-HISTORY

The unity of salvation-history in both the Old Testament and the New Testament consists in saving events, through which God speaks his word. The God of the Bible is a God who acts; and biblical theology, rightly understood, is the recital of the mighty acts of God:[1] "Who can utter the mighty doings of the Lord, or show forth all his praise" (Psa. 106:2) ; "The Lord has bared his holy arm before the eyes of all the nations; and all the ends of the earth shall see the salvation of our God" (Isa. 52: 10). But the acts of God are evident only to the eyes of faith, only when illuminated by inspired interpretation. Saving acts and inspired interpretation — the two together constitute the revelatory-redemptive process. God redeems, and in redemption he reveals himself. God speaks his word, and through his word he makes known his salvation.

This means that redemption is rooted in history. And the history with which the Bible is most concerned is the history of the covenant people. From the call of Abraham and the re-

---

[1] Cf. G. Ernest Wright, *God Who Acts* (London: SCM Press, 1956), especially Chapter II.

demption of the people of Israel from slavery in Egypt and the
election of them to be God's covenant people, to the life, death,
and resurrection of Jesus and the founding of the church as the
New Israel, the new covenant people, the theme is the same:
the people of God and the reign of God realized in and through
the covenant people.

The center of this redemptive history is the Christ-event —
the incarnation, life, teaching, death and resurrection of Jesus.
"And the word became flesh and dwelt among us . . ." (John
1:14). "In many and various ways God spoke of old to our
fathers by the prophets; but in these last days he has spoken to
us by a Son . . ." (Heb. 1:1). And the purpose of the incarnation
is revelation and redemption. "He who has seen me has seen the
Father" (John 14:9; cf. 1:14, 18; 12:45). "The Father has sent
his Son as the Savior of the world" (I John 4:14).

That the Christ-event is the center of salvation-history is
the central thesis of Oscar Cullmann's highly significant book,
Christ and Time. Cullmann conceives of salvation-history as an
upward sloping line, with Christ at the mid-point. All that
comes before him is fulfilled by him, while all that comes after
him is determined by him.

Cullmann speaks of a twofold movement in history embody-
ing the principles of election and representation.[2] From creation
to Christ the movement is one of reduction; from Christ onward
it is one of expansion. From fallen humanity God chooses
Israel as the instrument of salvation. When Israel as a nation
is unable to fulfill this mission, God's purpose narrows to the
remnant and from the remnant to one man. In Deutero-Isaiah
it is the Servant of the Lord; in Daniel it is the Son of Man.
Jesus of Nazareth enters into history and fulfills the mission of
the Suffering Servant of the Lord and the Danielic Son of Man.
"By his vicarious death he first completes that for which God
had chosen the people of Israel."[3] In Jesus redemptive history
has reached its center, and the movement is no longer from the
many to the one, but from the one to the many. "The Church
on earth, in which the Body of Christ is represented, plays in the
New Testament conception a central role for the redemption of

[2] Oscar Cullmann, *Christ and Time* (London: SCM Press, English translation, reprint, 1952), pp. 116-18.
[3] *Ibid.,* p. 116.

all mankind and thereby for the entire creation."[4] The movement from the many to the one is the old covenant, while the movement from the one to the many is the new covenant.

The saving action of God in history in its meaning for revelation is the basis of the eschatological hope of the New Testament. The Christ who has already come is the basis of our expectation of the Christ who will come again. Christ will bring to completion the work which he has already begun. "And I am sure that he who began a good work in you will bring it to completion at the day of Jesus Christ" (Phil. 1:6).

> That which has already happened offers the solid guarantee for that which will take place. *The hope of the final victory is so much the more vivid because of the unshakably firm conviction that the battle that decides the victory has already taken place.*[5]

The recognition of the unity of the biblical revelation as consisting of saving events, with the Christ-event at the center, is manifested also in the emphasis upon the *kerygma* in twentieth-century biblical and theological study. The noun *kerygma* comes from the verb *keryssein* meaning "to proclaim," to do the work of a *keryx,* a towncrier or herald. The noun *kerygma* can mean the act of proclamation or the thing proclaimed. In the New Testament the second meaning is the more common. Generally speaking, the *kerygma* is the event proclaimed (e.g., I Cor. 1:21; 15:14; Rom. 16:25). The new understanding of the *kerygma* is the result of the work of many scholars, but doubtless the most significant contribution is that made by C. H. Dodd in his epoch-making book, *The Apostolic Preaching and Its Developments.*

The thesis of Dodd, briefly stated, is this: imbedded in the epistles of Paul in such passages as Romans 1:2-5; 4:24-25; 10:8-9; I Corinthians 15:3-4 and perhaps Romans 8:31-34 are indications of a proclamation (*kerygma*) which did not have its origin with Paul but which is to be traced to the early days of the primitive church. When these passages are compared with the sermons of Peter in the early chapters of Acts (2:14-39; 3:12-26; 4:8-12; 10: 35-43), it is seen that there is a basic similarity in emphasis and thought forms. Says Dodd, "A comparison of Paul and Acts enables us to trace the essential elements in the apostolic Preach-

---

[4] *Ibid.,* pp. 117-18.
[5] *Ibid.,* p. 87. Italics in the original.

ing to a very early date indeed."[6] Dodd maintains that though
the sermons in Acts are not to be interpreted as verbatim re-
ports, nevertheless they are essentially trustworthy in determining
what the early *kerygma* was. Dodd's summary is as follows:

> First, the age of fulfilment has dawned. . . . 'The things which
> God foreshewed by the mouth of all the prophets, He thus
> fulfilled' (Acts 3:18) . . . . Secondly, this has taken place through
> the ministry, death, and resurrection of Jesus, of which a brief
> account is given, with proof from the Scriptures that all took
> place through 'the determinate counsel and foreknowledge
> of God.' . . . Thirdly, by virtue of the resurrection Jesus has
> been exalted at the right hand of God, as Messianic head of the
> new Israel. . . . Fourthly, the Holy Spirit in the Church is
> the sign of Christ's present power and glory. . . . Fifthly, the
> Messianic Age will shortly reach its consummation in the re-
> turn of Christ. . . . Finally, the *kerygma* always closes with an
> appeal for repentance, the offer of forgiveness and of the Holy
> Spirit, and the promise of 'salvation'. . . .[7]

This new understanding of the *kerygma* undermines the
thesis of nineteenth-century liberalism that Paul distorted the
gospel by substituting a gospel concerning Christ for a gospel of
the kingdom, by placing his emphasis upon the cross and the
resurrection of Christ rather than upon the ethical teachings
of Jesus. The sermons in Acts and the centrality given to the
passion narrative in the Gospel of Mark indicate that the early
church from the beginning understood that the center of the
gospel is in the saving action of God in Jesus the Christ.

The crucial point concerning the *kerygma,* as Stewart reminds
us, is that it was not dealing with abstractions, theories or gen-
eralities but with concrete actual events localized in space and
time. The apostles proclaimed not an idea of God, "but God
Himself in omnipotent action; not 'a doctrine of salvation,' but
salvation, the living deed; not a *Weltanschaung,* but Christ."[8]

This emphasis upon saving events as rooted in history gives
rise to what the theologians call "the scandal of particularity."
Why should God have revealed himself to Israel and not to some
other people? Why is the historical person, Jesus of Nazareth,

---

[6] C. H. Dodd, *The Apostolic Preaching and Its Developments* (London:
Hodder & Stoughton, first printed, 1936, eighth impression, 1956) , p. 56.

[7] *Ibid.,* pp. 21-23.

[8] James Stewart, *A Faith to Proclaim* (New York: Charles Scribner's
Sons, 1953) , p. 16.

to be interpreted as the Mediator of universal salvation? But "the scandal of particularity," C. H. Dodd reminds us,

> is inseparable from an historical revelation. History consists of events. An event happens *here* and not there, *now* and not then, to *this* person (or group) and not to that. And so the revelation of God in history came to one people and not to others, with the intention that through that people it should extend ultimately to all mankind.[9]

The unity of salvation-history is seen not only in the *fact* of saving events in history but in the *pattern of correspondence* between the events. Thus the exodus from Egypt was interpreted by the prophets as the type of the deliverance from the Babylonian exile (Jer. 16:14-15; Isa. 51:10-11). Even so the early Christians interpreted the deliverance from Egypt under Moses and the establishment of the covenant as types of the greater deliverance accomplished through the death and resurrection of Jesus and the establishment of the church. When Moses and Elijah appeared with Jesus on the mountain, the subject of their conversation was the exodus (*exodon*) which Jesus was to accomplish at Jerusalem (Luke 9:31). This dramatic departure (in death) came during the Passover Festival. And just as God through Moses gave to Israel the Passover Supper to commemorate their deliverance from Egypt, Jesus gave his disciples the Lord's Supper to commemorate their redemption from sin (Ex. 12; I Cor. 11:23-26; Matt. 26:26-29; Mark 14:22-25). Paul speaks of Christ as "our paschal lamb" (I Cor. 5:7), and the Fourth Gospel gives symbolic expression to this idea by representing the time of the crucifixion as the hour when the paschal lamb was slain (John 19:14; cf. I Pet. 1:18-19). Moreover, in the Fourth Gospel and the book of Acts Jesus is interpreted as the prophet like unto Moses (John 7:40; Acts 3:22-23; 7:37; cf. Deut. 18:15-19).[10]

---

[9] C. H. Dodd, *The Bible Today* (Cambridge University Press, 1956), p. 107.

[10] For a fuller treatment of the influence of the exodus idea upon the New Testament interpretation of salvation-history consult Herald Sahlin, "The New Exodus of Salvation According to St. Paul," *The Root of the Vine: Essays in Biblical Theology*, Anton Fridrichsen, editor (Westminster: Dacre Press, 1953), pp. 81-95; Otto A. Piper, "Unchanging Promises: Exodus in the New Testament," *Interpretation*, XI, January 1957, pp. 6-22; George L. Balentine, "Death of Jesus as a New Exodus," *Review and*

Implicit in the problem of the unity of salvation-history is
the relation of the old covenant to the new covenant, of the law
to the gospel, of the nation Israel to the church, of the Old
Testament to the New Testament. Briefly stated, the old is
preparation for the new, and the new is the fulfilment of the
old. If the old covenant had been sufficient, there would have
been no need for a new covenant. If the law could have brought
salvation, there would have been no room for the gospel. If
the nation Israel could have fulfilled God's purpose completely,
there would have been no reason for the church. If the Old
Testament had been final, there would have been no need for
the New Testament. But the old was provisional so that the
old covenant finds its fulfilment in the new covenant (Ex. 19:4-6;
Jer. 31:31-34; I Cor. 11:25; Heb. 8:6-13), the law in the gospel
(Matt. 5:17; Rom. 10:4), the nation Israel as the people of God
in the church as the people of God (Ex. 19:5-6; I Pet. 2:9-10),
the Old Testament in the New Testament (Rom. 15:4; II Cor.
1:20). We are no longer under the old covenant, but we are
under the new. We are no longer under the law as such, but
under the gospel. Israel, as a nation, is no longer the people
of God, for this role has now been assumed by the church. But
this does not mean that the Old Testament is no longer our
Bible because we now have the New Testament. The Old
Testament is the foundation; the New Testament is the building. A foundation without a building is pointless, but a building
without a foundation will not stand. The church in the first
few centuries of the Christian era wisely recognized this fact and
retained the Old Testament in the canon.

II. The Kingdom of God in the Proclamation of Jesus

When Jesus launched his public ministry in Galilee, he began
it with the proclamation: "The time is fulfilled, and the kingdom of God is at hand; repent, and believe in the gospel"
(Mark 1:15). With this emphasis upon the kingdom he sounded
what was to be the keynote of his entire ministry. "And he
went about all Galilee . . . preaching the gospel of the kingdom
. . . " (Matt. 4:23; cf. 9:35). "I must preach the good news of

---

Expositor, January 1962, pp. 27-41; Alan Richardson, *An Introduction to
the Theology of the New Testament* (New York: Harper & Row, Publishers,
1958), pp. 21-22; W. D. Davies, *The Setting of the Sermon on the Mount*
(Cambridge University Press, 1964), pp. 25-92.

the kingdom of God to the other cities also; for I was sent for this purpose" (Luke 4:43). References to the kingdom are prominent in all four sources of the Synoptic Gospels,[11] though they are conspicuously scarce in the Gospel of John.[12]

The kingdom of God was the heart of our Lord's message, his one, all-consuming passion. He represented it as of supreme value (Matt. 13:44-46), as worthy of any sacrifice (Mark 9:47), and as that which is to be sought above all else (Matt. 6:33; Luke 12:31). It was for the kingdom that he lived and for this that he died. And just as he began his public ministry proclaiming the kingdom of God, he ended it on the same note (Mark 14:25; Acts 1:3).[13]

In choosing the kingdom of God as the heart of his message and ministry Jesus was not selecting a concept foreign to Jewish ears, but one rooted in the Old Testament and cherished in the hearts of the Jews of his day. That God is King, the sovereign Lord of the universe, was one of the cardinal beliefs of Judaism. "For the Lord, the Most High, is terrible, a great king over all the earth" (Psa. 47:2). "The Lord has established his throne in the heavens, and his kingdom rules over all" (Psa. 103:19). "Thy kingdom is an everlasting kingdom, and thy dominion endures throughout all generations" (Psa. 145:13; cf. Dan. 4:3).

The fact that God's sovereignty is not always evident in human affairs in no way invalidated this faith. God is the eternal King, and his sovereignty is complete in heaven. Because of demonic and human rebellion, however, there are on earth forces inimical to God's will; and even Israel, God's chosen people, is temporarily under the domination of a foreign power. But there is coming a time when these limitations to God's sovereignty will be removed and his reign will be complete over all the earth.[14] This indomitable hope found expression in the prayer of the

[11] For an analysis of the sources see T. W. Manson, *The Teaching of Jesus* (Cambridge University Press, second edition revised, 1955), pp. 118-129.

[12] The passages are John 3:3, 5; 18:36 (*bis*).

[13] The centrality of the kingdom in the message of Jesus is uncontested, being affirmed even by the radical form critic, Rudolf Bultmann, *Jesus and the Word* (New York: Charles Scribner's Sons, 1934, 1958), pp. 27-56; *Theology of the New Testament* (New York: Charles Scribner's Sons, 1951), Vol. I, pp. 4-11 and by the post-Bultmannian scholar, Günther Bornkamm, *Jesus of Nazareth* (New York: Harper & Row, 1960), pp. 64-95.

[14] Clarence Tucker Craig, *The Beginning of Christianity* (New York: Abingdon Press, 1943), p. 78.

Kabbish, which Jews in Jesus' time prayed constantly (and even pray today): "May he establish his kingdom during your life and during your days, and during the life of all the house of Israel!"

Despite the certainty in the minds of the Jews concerning the ultimate triumph of the kingdom of God, there were nevertheless divergent views concerning the nature of the kingdom and how it was to be established. The Zealots interpreted the national hope in purely political terms. To them it was intolerable that the Jewish people should be subject to Roman domination as their forefathers in times past had been subject to the Syrians, Egyptians, Persians, Babylonians, and Assyrians. They longed for the re-establishment of the theocracy as it had existed in the good old days under King David. Moreover, they believed that as the Jews had triumphed over the Philistines under David and over the Syrians under the Maccabees they could even now triumph over the Romans if only the proper leader would appear and the people would rally to his cause.

The Pharisees believed that ultimately the coming of the kingdom depended upon God, but that he would establish his kingdom if only his people would be obedient to the law. They regarded the law as the revealed will of Yahweh, as perfect in every respect. Thus the expectation arose that the kingdom would come if only for two Sabbaths all of Israel would keep the law perfectly. In their minds the establishment of the kingdom would be an act of God, but it would come as a reward for Israel's obedience.

The apocalyptists, despairing of all human effort, believed that the kingdom would come only through a supernatural, catastrophic intervention on the part of God. It would be a supramundane kingdom which would come with the revelation of the Son of Man on the clouds of heaven (Dan. 7:13-14).

The crucial question is this: How did Jesus interpret the kingdom? Before this question can be answered two preliminary observations need to be made.

The first is that the Greek term *basileia* (kingdom) can mean either the territory ruled over by a king or the sovereignty, reign, or rule of a king. Nowadays it is regarded almost as axiomatic that in the discussion of the kingdom of God in the New Testament it is the second meaning with which we are dealing.

A second observation is that it is also almost axiomatic that the kingdom of God and the kingdom of heaven are synonymous terms. The term "kingdom of heaven" appears in the New Testament only in the Gospel of Matthew; and it is the term generally used in this gospel, though the term "kingdom of God" sometimes is used also. Since the two terms are used interchangeably in Matthew 19:23-24 and since in a number of passages in Matthew where "kingdom of heaven" is used parallel passages in Mark and Luke have "kingdom of God,"[15] the conclusion that the terms are synonymous expressions is almost inescapable.

Schmidt suggests that the term "kingdom of heaven" may carry the nuance of a lordship which comes down from heaven into this world. If this is the case, it further emphasizes the fact that the essential meaning of the kingdom is reign rather than realm and that it is a reign which comes not through human effort but through divine intervention.[16]

The controversial question in discussions of the kingdom of God in contemporary theology has to do with the relation of the kingdom to eschatology. Because this issue is extremely complicated only a cursory summary can be attempted here. Fortunately, however, this is all that is necessary since the subject has been treated frequently elsewhere.[17]

Nineteenth-century liberal theology, as expounded by Albrecht Ritschl and Adolf Harnack and as applied to the social gospel by Walter Rauschenbusch, tended to ignore the eschatological and apocalyptic elements in the gospels, treating the kingdom of God almost entirely apart from these considerations. Thus the kingdom of God was interpreted as "the organization of mankind through deeds proceeding out of the motive of love" and rooted in the redemption from guilt and the world

[15] Matt. 4:17=Mark 1:15; Matt. 8:11=Luke 13:29; Matt. 13:11=Mark 4:11; Matt. 19:23=Mark 10:23.

[16] Karl Ludwig Schmidt, "Basileia," *Theological Dictionary of the New Testament*, Gerhard Kittel, editor; Geoffrey W. Bromiley, translator and editor of the English edition (Grand Rapids: Wm. B. Eerdmans Publishing Company, 1964) , Vol. I, p. 582.

[17] For the history of the interpretation of the subject see Norman Perrin, *The Kingdom of God in the Teaching of Jesus* (Philadelphia: The Westminister Press, 1963) and Gösta Lundström, *The Kingdom of God in the Teaching of Jesus* (Richmond: John Knox Press, 1963) .

through Jesus,[18] as in Ritschl, or "the rule of the holy God in the hearts of individuals,"[19] as in Harnack, or "humanity organized according to the will of God" and as "a progressive reign of love in human affairs,"[20] as in Rauschenbusch. Interpreting the Jesus of history in terms of Kantian ethical idealism, this school tended to represent the kingdom of God as man's building project, a kind of social utopia, and to regard it as established by human cooperation with the will of God rather than by divine fiat from above.

Whereas the liberal theology described above had virtually excluded eschatology from consideration, Johannes Weiss and Albert Schweitzer interpreted Jesus against the background of Jewish apocalyptic and made eschatology the dominating concern. Schweitzer espoused a view which he called "thoroughgoing eschatology." According to this view, Jesus, dominated by Jewish apocalyptic expectations, predicted that the kingdom would come before the disciples completed the missionary journey recorded in Matthew 10 (cf. 10:23). When this did not happen, Jesus went up to Jerusalem determined to bring in the kingdom through his own death. But again the kingdom did not come. Schweitzer presents Jesus as a deluded apocalyptist, whose ethic was an interim ethic for the brief period between the present and the imminent coming of the kingdom of God. He overcomes the tendency to modernize Jesus inherent in the liberal reconstructions by presenting a Jesus who is out of all contact with modern man and thus irrelevant. Schweitzer himself, apparently aware of the problem, seeks to solve the difficulty by resorting to mysticism; but in doing so he virtually dissociates the Christ of faith from the Jesus of history.[21]

Reacting against both the noneschatological and the thoroughgoing eschatological interpretations and following leads sug-

18 Albrecht Ritschl, *Die christliche Lehre von der Rechtfertigung und Versohnung* (Bonn: Adolph Marcus, zweite verbesserte Auflage, 1883), III, S. 12-13.

19 Adolf Harnack, *What Is Christianity?* (G. P. Putnam's Sons, second edition revised, 1901), p. 60.

20 Walter Rauschenbusch, *A Theology for the Social Gospel* (New York: The Macmillan Company, 1918), p. 142.

21 Cf. Albert Schweitzer, *The Mystery of the Kingdom of God* (London: Adam & Black, 1950; first German edition, 1901) and *The Quest of the Historical Jesus* (New York: The Macmillan Company, 1961; first German edition, 1906).

gested by Ernst von Dobschutz[22] and Rudolf Otto,[23] C. H. Dodd interprets Jesus' view of the kingdom in terms of "realized eschatology." This he defines as "the impact upon this world of the 'powers of the world to come' in a series of events, unprecedented and unrepeatable, now in actual process."[24] Emphasizing passages of Scripture which he regards as unmistakably presenting the kingdom of God as a present reality,[25] he makes these normative for his whole interpretation. By excising some eschatological passages by means of the scissors of form criticism and by stressing the essentially symbolical character of the apocalyptic references which he retains, he virtually eliminates futuristic eschatology from the teaching of Jesus.

Whatever we may think of Schweitzer's reconstruction, this much we must acknowledge: he has made it impossible for us to interpret the kingdom of God in strictly noneschatological terms. Does this mean then that we are faced with the alternative of a kingdom that is altogether future, as in Schweitzer, or one that is altogether present, as in Dodd? We emphatically reject this either/or. Our position is that in the teaching of Jesus the kingdom of God is rooted in the eternal sovereignty of God; that it is manifested in history in acts that reveal the divine sovereignty, particularly in the Christ-event, and is thus a present reality; but that it reaches its consummation in the future in the supramundane world that will be disclosed at the second advent (*parousia*) of Jesus Christ. We believe that this is a position in keeping with the New Testament witness, and that only by arbitrary exegesis can one arrive at the interpretation of the kingdom as either exclusively future or exclusively present.

The biblical basis for the assertion that the kingdom of God is rooted in the eternal sovereignty of God has already been given, and this calls for no further elaboration. It is necessary now, however, to establish the exegetical basis for the assertion

22 Ernst von Dobschutz, *The Eschatology of the Gospels* (London, 1910).

23 Rudolf Otto, *The Kingdom of God and the Son of Man* (London: Lutterworth Press, 1938).

24 C. H. Dodd, *The Parables of the Kingdom* (London: Nisbet & Co., third edition, 1936), p. 51; cf. also *The Apostolic Preaching and its Developments*.

25 E.g., Mark 1:14-15; Matt. 12:28=Luke 11:20; Matt. 12:41-42=Luke 11:31-32.

that the kingdom of God in the teaching of Jesus as mediated to us by the Synoptic Gospels is both present and future.[26]

Perhaps the clearest illustration of the kingdom of God conceived as a present reality is the famous Q passage: "But if it is by the finger of God that I cast out demons, then the kingdom of God has come upon you" (Luke 11:20 = Matt. 12:28).[27] Here the RSV translation of the Greek verb *ephthasen* as "has come" is unquestionably correct.[28] When Jesus declares: ". . . something greater than Solomon is here . . . something greater than Jonah is here" (Luke 11:31-32 = Matt.12:41-42, Q), it is clear that he is speaking of the present reality of the kingdom.[29] The natural interpretation of Luke 16:16 is that Jesus is interpreting the era of the law and the prophets as ending with John and the era of the kingdom of God as beginning with himself. That the age of fulfilment — the age of the kingdom — has already dawned may surely be inferred from the words of Jesus to the effect that the disciples are blessed because they are even now hearing and seeing the fulfilment of promises for which the prophets and righteous men of old longed, but which were never realized in their day (Matt. 13:16-17 = Luke 10:23-24, Q).[30] Jesus' reply to messengers from John the Baptist fits into this pattern:

> Go and tell John what you hear and see: the blind receive their sight and the lame walk, lepers are cleansed and the deaf hear, and the dead are raised up, and the poor have good news

[26] For interpretations of the kingdom in the teaching of Jesus as both present and future see T. W. Manson, *op. cit.*, pp. 116-284, particularly pp. 40-41; C. J. Cadoux, *The Historic Mission of Jesus* (New York: Harper & Row), pp. 105-329; W. G. Kümmel, *Promise and Fulfilment* (London: SCM Press, 1957), *passim;* and Eric Rust, *Salvation History* (Richmond: John Knox Press, 1962), pp. 157-70. In the exegesis that follows no attempt is made to be exhaustive.

[27] Matt. 12:28 has "the Spirit of God." For the argument for the originality of "the finger of God" see Manson, *op. cit.*, pp. 82-83.

[28] Reginald H. Fuller, who maintains that the kingdom of God in the teaching of Jesus is exclusively future, recognizes the correctness of this translation. Fuller insists, however, that this is an example of the familiar prophetic device of speaking of a future event as if it were already present. In reality what is present is not the kingdom itself but only the signs of the kingdom (*The Mission and Achievement of Jesus* [London: SCM Press, 1954], pp. 25-27). This strikes us as an example of arbitrary exegesis.

[29] The RSV correctly translates the neuter pronoun *pleion* as "something."

[30] The passage in Luke reads "kings" instead of "righteous men."

preached to them. And blessed is he who takes no offense at me
(Matt. 11:4-6; cf. Isa. 35:5-6).

When Jesus declares: ". . . the kingdom of God is in the midst
of you"[31] (Luke 17:21), he can make this affirmation because he
is present and he embodies the kingdom.

Clear as are the references to the kingdom as a present reality,
equally clear are the passages which speak of it as future. In
our sources the ultimate triumph of the kingdom of God is connected with the *parousia* (coming) of the Son of Man (Luke
21:27, 31).[32] Various aspects of this *parousia* and the future
consummation of all things are delineated in the parables of
the Ten Virgins (Matt. 25:1-13), the Talents (Matt. 25:14-30;
cf. Luke 19:12-27), and the Last Judgment (Matt. 25:31-46).

A number of passages employ the figure of the messianic banquet in depicting the ultimate triumph of the kingdom. "And
men will come from east and west, and from north and south,
and sit at table in the kingdom of God" (Luke 13:29 = Matt.
8:11, Q). The messianic banquet idea is present in the parable
of the Great Supper in both its Matthean and Lucan versions
(Matt. 22:1-10; Luke 14:16-24). In both of these accounts, however, it is the response to the gospel invitation in the present
that determines participation in the messianic banquet in the
future. After instituting the Lord's Supper Jesus says to his
disciples, "Truly, I say unto you, I shall not drink again of the
fruit of the vine until that day when I drink it new in the kingdom of God" (Mark 14:25; cf. Luke 22:16, 18). Here Jesus
interprets the Last Supper with the disciples as an anticipation
of the messianic banquet in the kingdom of God.

In the parables of Jesus emphasis at times is laid on the present
aspect of the kingdom and at times on the future manifestation,
though both ideas seem to be included in some parables. That
the kingdom is a present reality, divine and mysterious, exer-

[31] The words *entos humon* may also be translated "within you," but this
translation would not eliminate the idea implicit in the passage that the
kingdom is a present reality. Most scholars prefer the translation "in the
midst of you" or "in your midst."

[32] This is a part of the famous eschatological discourse recorded in Mark
13, Matthew 24, and Luke 21. An adequate treatment of the problems
raised by this one passage would require a book. Indeed, G. R. Beasley-
Murray has written two books about this discourse: *Jesus and the Future*
(London: Macmillan & Co., 1954) and *A Commentary on Mark 13* (London:
Macmillan & Co., 1957).

cising its force in the world, is suggested by the parables of the
Seed Growing of Itself (Mark 4:26-29), the Mustard Seed (Mark
4:30-32), and the Leaven (Matt. 13:33). The future consummation receives emphasis in the parables of the Tares (Matt. 13:
24-30), the Dragnet (Matt. 13:47-48), and the Sower (Mark
4:1-9). In these parables it is customary to focus exclusive emphasis upon either the present reality of the kingdom[33] or upon
its future consumation.[34] However, since both of these emphases
are present in the teaching of Jesus, why not allow for a dual
interpretation of such parables as the Seed Growing of Itself
(Mark 4:26-28), the Tares (Matt. 13:24-30), and the Sower
(Mark 4:1-9)?

There are in the Synoptic Gospels, as we shall see, passages
which, while referring to the kingdom of God as future, do not
seem to have reference to the consummation of all things but
which seem to anticipate a more imminent fulfilment, a fulfilment within human history and not beyond it. Mark 1:15
probably belongs to this category. Despite Dodd's attempt to
prove that *engiken* in this passage has the force of "arrived"
and that the passage should be translated: "The kingdom of
God has come . . . ,"[35] it is doubtful if Dodd's arguments will
bear the weight of close examination; and the RSV rendering:
"The kingdom of God is at hand. . . ." appears to be the better
translation.[36]

In Mark 9:1 Jesus says: "Truly, I say to you, there are some
standing here who will not taste death before they see the kingdom of God come with power." Probably the key to the interpretation of this passage is the words "come with power."
The passage is interpreted apocalyptically in Matthew (16:28):
"the Son of man coming in his kingdom," and the words "with
power" are dropped in Luke (9:27). But in its original setting
it seems to be a prediction of the powerful manifestation of the
sovereignty of God to be accomplished through the crucifixion,
the resurrection, the coming of the Spirit, and the emergence
of the church as the community witnessing to God's acts of redemption in Christ.

33 As in Dodd, *The Parables of the Kingdom,* pp. 175-94.
34 As in Fuller, *op. cit.,* pp. 44-45.
35 Dodd, *The Parables of the Kingdom,* p. 44.
36 See Fuller, *op. cit.,* pp. 21-25 and Kümmel, *op. cit.,* pp. 23-25. Matt.
10:7 and Luke 10:9, 10 also belong to the same category as Mark 1:15.

The shadow of the cross fell across our Lord's path from the beginning of his ministry, for from the time of his baptism in the Jordan and his temptations in the wilderness he had come to interpret his essential mission in terms of the fulfilment of the Servant ideal of Isaiah 53.[37] According to Luke, when the risen Christ appeared unto his disciples, he opened their minds to understand the Scriptures, explaining:

> Thus it is written, that the Christ should suffer and on the third day rise from the dead, and that repentance and forgiveness of sins should be preached in his name to all nations, beginning from Jerusalem. You are witnesses of these things (Luke 24: 46-48).

Here a distinct connection is made between the death and resurrection of the Christ on the one hand and the commission to preach forgiveness of sins in his name to all nations on the other.

As the one who always abode in the Father's will, Jesus interpreted his entire ministry in terms of the manifestation of the sovereignty of God. Thus he could speak of the kingdom as already present in his teaching and in his ministry of healing and exorcising demons. Yet Jesus anticipated an even more striking manifestation of the sovereignty of God which would take place before the final triumph of the kingdom of God and the consummation of all things. He believed in a God who would bring triumph out of tragedy and who would manifest his sovereignty even in the most heinous of all crimes, in that which from a human point of view would seem to be the ultimate denial of God's reign. Never did he regard himself as a pawn in human hands, a victim of circumstances beyond his control. He interpreted his coming death as the cup which he had to drink (Mark 10:38; cf. John 18:11) and as the baptism of which the baptism in the Jordan was but a foretaste (Mark 10:38; Luke 12:50). All would happen not according to human caprice, but in keeping with God's plan and according to his timetable (Luke 13:31-33). Moreover, our Lord seems to have had the prophetic insight to understand that his death and resurrection would accomplish that which his ministry of teaching and

---

[37] Evidence for this will be presented in the next section, which is entitled "The Dominance of the Servant Ideal."

healing could never effect. This would be the coming of the
kingdom "with power."[38]

Fuller points out that the Gospel of Mark is historically correct in making Caesarea Philippi a turning point in the story
of Jesus.

> From that point onwards Jesus turns from the public proclama-
> tion of the advent of the Reign of God and addresses himself to
> the private initiation of his disciples into the mystery of his im-
> pending death. This mystery is that Jesus has been sent not
> only to announce the coming Reign of God, but to perform the
> decisive event through which God will inaugurate that Reign.
> This decisive event Jesus conceives in terms of the fulfilment
> of the vocation of the Suffering Servant of Isaiah.[39]

The kingdom of God is a divine gift (Luke 12:32), not a
human achievement. Man cannot build it or establish it; neither
can he bring it. He can only seek it (Matt. 6:33 = Luke 12:31),
wait for it (Mark 15:43), enter it (Mark 9:47; Matt. 18:3),
and receive it like a child (Mark 10:15). The kingdom is a
present reality, and yet one is to pray for its coming (Luke 11:
2 = Matt. 6:10, Q). The kingdom of God is the sovereignty of
God. It involves the doing of God's will on earth as in heaven
(Matt. 6:10).

The kingdom of God is manifest in Jesus, who not only embodies the sovereignty of God but mediates it as well. Just as
one's relation to Jesus determines his relation to the Father
(Luke 10:22 = Matt. 11:27, Q), one's relation to Jesus likewise
determines his relation to the kingdom. The kind of absolute
devotion which Jesus demanded toward the kingdom (Matt.
6:33 = Luke 12:31; Matt. 13:44-46; Mark 9:47) is the same kind
of devotion that he expected toward himself (Matt. 10:37-38 =
Luke 14:26-27; Mark 8:34; Luke 9:57-62 = Matt. 8:19-22). To
lose one's life or renounce all for Jesus' sake, the gospel's sake,

---

[38] The declaration of our Lord in the Fourth Gospel: "Now is the judgment of this world, now shall the ruler of this world be cast out; and I,
when I am lifted up from the earth, will draw all men to myself" (John
12:31-32) is fully consistent with the Synoptic witness.

[39] Fuller, op. cit., p. 77. It is Fuller's desire to make absolutely clear
"the cruciality of the cross" (p. 49) which leads him to interpret all references to the kingdom in the teaching of Jesus as from Jesus' standpoint yet
future. The cruciality of the cross in the mind of our Lord can be
established, however, without resorting to strained exegesis.

and the kingdom's sake are all one and the same thing (Mark 8:35; 10:29 = Matt. 19:29 = Luke 18:29).

Since the kingdom does not operate in a vacuum, implicit within the concept of the kingdom is that of the church, the people of God, the little flock unto whom the Father gives the kingdom (Luke 12:32). Entrance into the kingdom is determined not by wealth (Luke 6:20; Mark 10:23), nor by human wisdom (Mark 10:14-15), nor by race (Matt. 8:11-12), nor by righteousness as judged by Jewish legal standards (Matt. 5:20; 21:31), but by a willingness to submit to God's righteousness, to enter the kingdom on God's terms (Mark 10:14-15).

The earliest church correctly perceived the centrality of Christ in God's plan of redemption. Hunter has called our attention to the fact that the message which the earliest church proclaimed echoed that of Jesus. According to Mark 1:14-15 Jesus had proclaimed: (1) The time is fulfilled. (2) The kingdom of God is at hand. (3) Therefore, repent and believe. According to the *kerygma* in Acts the apostles proclaimed: (1) The prophecies are fulfilled. (2) The new age has come with the fact of Christ. (3) Therefore, repent and believe. In both proclamations (1) and (3) are the same. However, in the apostles' proclamation the life, death, and resurrection of Jesus have replaced the proclamation of the kingdom of God. Does this not show that the earliest church perceived that in proclaiming Christ it was proclaiming the kingdom?[40]

Another line of evidence pointing in the same direction is the fact that whereas the Synoptic Gospels present a Christ who proclaimed the kingdom, the Fourth Gospel presents a Christ who proclaims himself. This means that to proclaim Christ is to proclaim the kingdom and to receive Christ is to receive the kingdom.

Perceiving the fact that the apostolic preaching of Christ took the place of Christ's own preaching of the kingdom, Forsyth interprets this to mean that through the redemptive triumph of his death and resurrection Christ became identified with the kingdom in an even more striking manner than before his death. "Nothing in his life served the kingdom like his manner of leaving it."[41] By his death he became the kingdom

---

40 A. M. Hunter, *Introducing New Testament Theology* (London: SCM Press, 1957), p. 24, n. 2.

41 P. T. Forsyth, *The Person and Place of Jesus Christ* (London: Independent Press, 1961, first edition, 1909), p. 122.

with the natural consequence that the gospel of Christ took the place formerly occupied by the gospel of the kingdom.

III. THE DOMINANCE OF THE SERVANT IDEAL

The gospels record only one instance in which Jesus quoted directly from the Servant Songs: "For I tell you that this scripture must be fulfilled in me, 'And he was reckoned with transgressors'; for what is written about me has its fulfillment" (Luke 22:37 = Isa. 53:12). This one quotation, however, is highly significant, because it suggests not only that Jesus regarded his mission as that of fulfilling the Servant ideal but that he also understood identification with sinners as the method of fulfilment. It was precisely this fact — Jesus' identification of himself with sinners, particularly the down and out and those neglected by official Judaism which brought him into the sharpest conflict with the Jewish religious authorities (e.g., Mark 2:15-17; Luke 15). Identification with sinners was, of course, only one element in the conflict; but probably it was the chief one. Jesus' identification with sinners evoked opposition, which resulted in suffering on the part of Jesus. And this suffering itself became the means through which Jesus fulfilled the role of the Suffering Servant, who was to effect redemption through vicarious suffering.

It is impossible to say exactly when Jesus first began to think of his mission in terms of identification with sinners and the fulfilment of the Servant ideal. There is strong evidence, however, that at least from the time of his baptism he thought of his mission in this way.

It was probably a deep sense of mission, born of a unique filial consciousness, which brought Jesus to the Jordan to be baptized by John. This filial consciousness was confirmed and deepened and the nature of the mission clarified by the voice from heaven: "Thou art my beloved Son; with thee I am well pleased" (Mark 1:11). It has frequently been pointed out that this voice brings together two well-known passages from the Old Testament, namely, Psalm 2:7 and Isaiah 42:1. The first of these two passages "constitutes the *coronation formula* of the messianic king who sits on Israel's throne," while the second passage "represents the *ordination formula* of the Suffering Servant of the Lord."[42] Thus two streams of Old Testament prophecy which heretofore had been separate are united, and it is suggested that Jesus is to fulfill the highest spiritual ideals of the Davidic king by accepting the mission and method of the Suffering Servant. The Father's will for the Son is that he should be a suffering Messiah.[43]

In submitting to a baptism defined as "a baptism of repentance for the forgiveness of sins" (Luke 3:3) Jesus, the sinless one, was already *"numbering Himself with transgressors,* submitting to be baptized with their baptism, identifying Himself with them in their relation to God as sinners, making all their responsibilities His own."[44]

---

[42] John Wick Bowman, *The Intention of Jesus* (Philadelphia: Westminster Press, 1943), pp. 38-39. Italics in the original.

[43] The statements in the New Testament indicating that the idea of a suffering Messiah was contrary to the expectation of the Jews in the first century and a stumbling block to them constitute a strong argument for the idea that the ideal of the messianic king of the Davidic line had not been fused with the Suffering Servant ideal of Deutero-Isaiah before the time of Jesus. Cf. Matt. 16:21-23; Mark 8:31; 9:31; Luke 24:19-21; Acts 17:3; I Cor. 1:23; Gal. 5:11. However, in recent years there has been a growing tendency on the part of biblical scholars to argue that fusion of these two streams antedates Jesus. Cf. W. D. Davies, *Paul and Rabbinic Judaism* (London: S.P.C.K., 1955), pp. 274-84; I. Engnell, "The 'Ebed Yahweh Songs and the Suffering Messiah in Deutero-Isaiah,'" *Bulletin of the John Rylands Library*, 31, 1948, pp. 3-42; Aage Bentzen, *King and Messiah* (London: Lutterworth Press, 1955), pp. 48-72. Engnell interprets the Servant as a royal figure, whereas Bentzen regards the Servant as the Messiah, but a Messiah of the Mosaic rather than the Davidic type. For an answer to the attempt to find a fusion of these two streams prior to the time of Jesus see H. H. Rowley, *The Servant of the Lord and Other Essays on the Old Testament* (London: Lutterworth Press, 1952), Chapter II, "The Suffering Servant and the Davidic Messiah." The problem is indeed a complicated one, but the evidence seems to lie on the side of those who regard the fusion of the two streams of prophecy as having been made for the first time by Jesus or by the voice from heaven addressed to Jesus. Cf. Bowman, *op. cit.*, pp. 35-40; Alan Richardson, *An Introduction to the Theology of the New Testament* (New York: Harper and Row, 1958), p. 136; H. Wheeler Robinson, *Redemption and Revelation* (London: Nisbet & Co., 1947), p. 199; Rowley, *op. cit.* For an able defense of the idea that Jesus interpreted his role in terms of the fulfilment of the Suffering Servant ideal consult Reginald H. Fuller, *The Mission and Achievement of Jesus* (London: SCM Press, first published, 1954). For an interpretation which minimizes the influence of the Servant conception in the New Testament consult Morna D. Hooker, *Jesus and the Servant* (London: S.P.C.K., 1959).

[44] James Denny, *The Death of Christ,* edited by R. V. G. Tasker (London: The Tyndale Press, 1951), p. 22.

The other Jews went to John the Baptist to be baptized for their own sins. But when Jesus is baptized just as all the others were, he hears a divine voice which implicitly says to him, 'You are not baptized for your own sins, but for those of the whole people. For you are the one whose vicarious suffering for the sins of others the prophet predicted.'[45]

When John expressed a hesitancy to baptize Jesus, Jesus responded, "Let it be so now; for thus it is fitting for us to fulfill all righteousness" (Matt. 3:15). In these words there is probably an echo of Isaiah 53:11 in which the Servant of the Lord justifies many by bearing their iniquities.[46] Later, according to Mark 10:39 and Luke 12:50, Jesus spoke of his coming death as a baptism.

The Synoptic Gospels all indicate that following his baptism Jesus underwent a period of severe temptation in the wilderness, but only Matthew and Luke are detailed enough in their accounts to give an indication of the nature of the temptations and some hint as to their meaning (Matt. 4:1-11 = Luke 4:1-13). Jesus already had accepted for himself the role of a suffering Messiah. In opposition to this, Satan tried to allure Jesus by bringing before his mind the popular expectation concerning the Messiah and suggesting ways by which he could receive immediate recognition. There is every indication that there was a severe struggle, but Jesus emerged victorious. He rejected the economic approach, the political approach, and the spectacular religious approach to messiahship, refusing to be deflected from God's purpose that he should fulfill his mission through suffering.

Near the beginning of his public ministry Jesus returned to Nazareth, his native village, and entering the synagogue read from Isaiah 61:1-2, interpreting the words as fulfilled in himself (Luke 4:16-21). This passage in Isaiah, though not one of the Servant Songs, belongs to the same circle of ideas as the Servant Songs, and may be used as evidence that Jesus had accepted for himself the mission of the Suffering Servant.

The reference to the removal of the bridegroom in Mark 2:20 is difficult to date in the ministry of Jesus because it belongs to a passage in Mark which probably is arranged topically

45 Oscar Cullmann, *The Christology of the New Testament* (London: SCM Press, 1959), p. 67.

46 Alfred E. Garvie, *Studies in the Inner Life of Jesus* (New York: George H. Doran Company, 1907), p. 125.

rather than chronologically. The significance of this passage in relation to the Suffering Servant ideal is that it contains a veiled prediction by Jesus of his coming death. It was an enigmatic statement, which the disciples probably did not understand until after the resurrection.

Of decisive importance for an understanding of Jesus' interpretation of his mission is Mark 8:27-38 (cf. parallels in Matt. 16:13-28; Luke 9:18-27). A study of this passage yields the formula: Jesus = Christ = Son of Man = Suffering Servant. Upon being confessed as the Christ, Jesus immediately begins to speak of himself as the Son of Man; but he interprets the mission of the Son of Man in terms of that of the Suffering Servant. Jesus enjoined his disciples to tell no one about him — that is, that he was the Christ (Mark 8:30 = Matt. 16:21 = Luke 9:20) — because of the mistaken political and military associations of the term in the popular expectation.[47]

Jesus, as was his custom, avoided the term "Christ" in speaking of himself, using instead his favorite self-designation, "the Son of Man." This was a term with enough ambiguity to enable Jesus to pour into it the meaning that he desired. Jesus interpreted the mission of the Son of Man both in terms of the suffering of the Servant of the Servant Songs and in terms of the exaltation of the Son of Man in Daniel 7 (Mark 8:31, 38).

Mark 8:31 sets forth the first clear prediction by Jesus of his coming death and resurrection. "The word 'must' (dei) indicates that Jesus saw His suffering, death, and rising again as in-

---

47 Some scholars deny completely the messianic consciousness of Jesus, maintaining that Jesus did not claim to be the Messiah, nor was he recognized as such until after the resurrection. Traces of the messianic consciousness of Jesus in the gospels, according to this point of view, are a reflection of the faith of the early church in Jesus as the Christ, not genuine history. Cf. W. Wrede, *Das Messiasgeheimnis in den Evangelien* (Göttingen, 1901, 2nd ed., 1913); F. C. Grant, *The Gospel of the Kingdom*, (New York: The Macmillan Company, 1940), pp. 63-64, 157; Rudolf Bultmann, *Theology of the New Testament* (New York: Charles Scribner's Sons, 1951), Vol. I, pp. 26-32; Günther Bornkamm, *Jesus of Nazareth* (New York: Harper & Row, 1960), pp. 169-178. The crucial question is whether radical form criticism has made it impossible to accept the essential reliability of the Gospel of Mark. It is the writer's contention that it has not. Cf. C. H. Dodd, *New Testament Studies* (Manchester: The University Press, 1953), pp. 1-11; T. W. Manson, *Studies in the Gospels and the Epistles*, edited by Matthew Black (Manchester: The University Press, 1962), pp. 3-12, 23-27; Vincent Taylor, *The Gospel According to St. Mark* (London: Macmillan & Co., 1952), pp. 130-149; and Taylor, *Jesus and His Sacrifice*, pp. 82-163.

ward and divinely conditioned necessities."[48] That Jesus had accepted for himself the fulfilment of the role of the Suffering Servant is the most plausible explanation of such a passage. Peter's protest against Jesus' interpretation indicates how deeply rooted was the popular expectation, even in the hearts of the disciples, and how foreign to their expectation was the idea of a suffering Messiah. Jesus recognized Peter's protest as a Satanic temptation such as he had experienced in the wilderness, and he quickly brushed it aside (cf. also John 6:15). Jesus then boldly stated that those who would be his disciples must be willing to identify themselves with him in humiliation and suffering, thus finding room for a corporate aspect in the fulfilment of the Servant ideal.

Other predictions by Jesus of his coming death and resurrection are found in Mark 9:31 and 10:33-34. Many scholars interpret these predictions, along with that in Mark 8:31, as predictions after the event. It is possible that some of the details have been heightened on the basis of a knowledge of the actual course of events. However, there is nothing in these passages which Jesus, through identification with the Suffering Servant ideal, relating it to other Old Testament passages (e.g., Hos. 6:2), and interpreting the course of events already in progress with prophetic insight, could not have foretold. The animosity of the Jewish leaders toward him would surely issue in his death. But since the Jews did not have the authority to put a man to death, this execution would be carried out by the Roman authorities. The details of mocking, spitting, and scourging were probably suggested by Isaiah 50:6.

Jesus repudiated the selfish ambitions of James and John by appealing to the Servant ideal of true greatness as determined by service (Mark 10:35-44). Then he related this ideal to his own mission with the words: "For the Son of man also came not to be served but to serve, and to give his life as a ransom for many" (Mark 10:45; cf. Matt. 20:28). The genuineness of the words, "to give his life a ransom for many," has often been questioned, the usual argument being that Pauline ideas are being read into the teachings of Jesus. But there are good reasons for accepting the genuineness of the saying,[49] and the passage makes good sense when interpreted against the background of Isaiah

---

[48] Taylor, *Jesus and His Sacrifice*, p. 90.
[49] Cf. Taylor, *Jesus and His Sacrifice*, pp. 97-105.

53 and Psalm 49:7-8. The words "to give his life" and "for many" seem clearly to be echoes from Isaiah 53. Though the word "ransom" (*lutron*) does not occur in Isaiah 53, the idea of a ransom harmonizes well with the fourth Servant Song (especially 53:5).

Three words of Jesus spoken at the Last Supper reflect the influence of the Servant ideal upon Jesus' understanding of his mission. Luke 22:37 has already been mentioned. "But I am among you as one who serves" (Luke 22:27) is another.[50] The third is "This is my blood of the covenant, which is poured out for many" (Mark 14:24; cf. Matt. 26:28; Luke 22:20; I Cor. 11: 24). Passages like Exodus 19:4-6; 24:3-11; and Jeremiah 31:34 are doubtless also in the background of this passage. But the influence of the Servant Songs is suggested in the words "for many" and "covenant." Representation and covenant were two main elements of the work of the Servant. Isaiah 53 emphasizes representation in the use of such words as "for" and "instead of." And the Servant's task of re-establishing the covenant is mentioned in Isaiah 42:6 and 49:8.[51]

When following his resurrection Jesus opened the minds of his disciples to understand the Scriptures, saying to them, "Thus it is written, that the Christ should suffer and on the third day rise from the dead . . ." (Luke 24:45-46), who can doubt that Isaiah 53 was one of the chief passages of which he made use?

The book of Acts indicates that in the most ancient period of early Christianity the person and work of Christ were interpreted according to the Servant of the Lord Christology.[52] The Ethiopian eunuch, who had been reading Isaiah 53:7f., asked Philip, "About whom, pray, does the prophet say this, about himself or about some one else?" Thereupon, "Philip opened his mouth, and beginning with this scripture he told him the good news of Jesus" (Acts 8:26-35). Four times in the book of Acts Jesus is called Servant (3:13, 26; 4:27, 30). The Greek word is *pais,* the same word generally used in the Septuagint to translate *ebed Yahweh* (the Servant of the Lord) in the Servant Songs of Deutero-Isaiah. Cullmann speaks of *pais* in these passages as a Christological title: "Jesus is called *Pais* exactly

[50] Cf. Jesus washing his disciples' feet, John 13:1-15.
[51] Oscar Cullmann, *The Christology of the New Testament* (London: SCM Press, first English edition, 1959), pp. 64-65.
[52] *Ibid.,* p. 73.

as he later is commonly called 'Christ.' "[53] The influence of the
Servant Songs is seen also in Acts 3:14; 7:52; and 22:14 in the
use of the term *dikaios* (righteous) with reference to Jesus as
the Servant.[54]

Cullmann calls attention to the fact that of the four instances
in which Jesus is called *pais* the first two are in a sermon by
Peter and the second two are in prayers offered while Peter is
present.[55] He sees this as evidence of the fact that Peter, for
whom the idea of a suffering Christ had been a stumbling
block, now had come not only to accept but to glory in the
sufferings and death of Jesus and to make them central in his
explanation of Jesus' earthly work. Cullmann calls attention also
to the influence of Peter in the use made of the Servant ideal in
I Peter 2:21-25 (regardless of whether Peter is the author or not)
and in the use of the *ebed Yahweh* concept in the Markan tradition (provided Papias is correct in "connecting the oral tradition behind the Gospel of Mark with the preaching of
Peter").[56]

The influence of the Servant conception is also discernible
in the epistles of Paul. I Corinthians 15:3-4 is definitely based
on the primitive *kerygma* and the same is probably the case with
Romans 4:25. Both passages, however, reflect the influence of
the Servant conception. II Corinthians 5:21 refers to Isaiah
53:6. The influence of the Servant ideal is evident also in Phi-
lippians 2:7-8 and Romans 5:19.[57] Paul twice quotes directly the
fourth Servant Song (Rom. 10:16 = Isa. 53:1; Rom. 15:21 = Isa.
52:15), but neither quotation has any bearing upon his interpretation of the death of Christ.

The designation of Jesus as "the Lamb of God, who takes
away the sin of the world" in John 1:29 (cf. 1:36) is assuredly
to be interpreted as a reference to Isaiah 53. Jeremias[58] thinks
that behind the phrase "the Lamb of God" in this passage is an
Aramaic construction of *ebed Yahweh*.[59]

Twenty-seven times in the Apocalypse the term "Lamb" is

53 *Loc. cit.*
54 *Ibid.*; cf. Isa. 53:11.
55 *Ibid.*, p. 74.
56 *Loc. cit.*
57 Cf. Cullmann, *op. cit.*, pp. 76-77, 161-64.
58 W. Zimmerli and J. Jeremias, *The Servant of God* (London: SCM
Press, 1957) , p. 82.
59 Cf. Cullmann, *op. cit.*, p. 71.

used with reference to Christ. The choice of the term *arnion* instead of the usual term for lamb, *amnos,* is probably to be explained on the basis of its assonance with *therion,* "wild beast."[60] There are sacrificial overtones in the usage of *arnion* in the Apocalypse, but the dominant ideas expressed are those related to the Servant of the Lord concept. The ideas in the fifth chapter of suffering, "as though it had been slain" (5:6), salvation, "didst ransom men for God" (5:9), and glory, expressed in the idea of the proximity of the Lamb to the throne (5:6), are key ideas in the fourth Servant Song.[61] These ideas, along with the inclusion of the Gentiles, "from every tribe and tongue and people and nation" (5:9), make the impression of the influence of the Servant ideal overwhelming. Moreover, in the designation of Christ in one passage as "the Lion of the tribe of Judah, the Root of David," and "the Lamb," there is a fusion of the idea of the messianic king and the Suffering Servant (5:5-6).[62]

Other references to the Servant Songs are found in Hebrews 9:28 and in Matthew 8:17 and 12:17-21.

In summary, though the term "Servant" never becomes a major Christological title in the New Testament such as "Christ" or "Lord," the influence of the Servant ideal is evident throughout the New Testament, particularly in the Synoptic Gospels; and the Servant ideal supplies one of the major keys for an intepretation of the atonement in the New Testament.

IV. THE ATONEMENT AND GOD

The early sermons in Acts represent the crucifixion of Jesus as the crime of the Jews which God overruled for his glory by raising Jesus from the dead (Acts 2:23-24, 36; 3:13-15; 4:10; 5:30; 7:52; 10:39-40). And yet, paradoxical as it is, these same sermons make it clear that Jesus' death did not occur by accident but "according to the definite plan and foreknowledge of God" (Acts 2:23; cf. 3:18; 4:27-28).

Because Paul understood God's redemptive purpose in the

---

[60] C. Ryder Smith, *The Bible Doctrine of Salvation* (London: The Epworth Press, revised edition, 1946), p. 192.

[61] Smith, *op. cit.,* p. 193.

[62] Cf. Vincent Taylor, *The Atonement in New Testament Teaching* (London: The Epworth Press, second edition, reprint, 1946), p. 36.

death of Christ he could speak of Christ crucified as "the power of God and the wisdom of God" (I Cor. 1:24), and he could speak of the death of Christ as "according to the will of our God and Father" (Gal. 1:4). For the same reason he gloried in the cross and made it the center of his message (Gal. 6:14; I Cor. 2:2). Likewise Peter, after speaking of the precious blood of Christ as the price of our redemption, went on to say: "He was destined before the foundation of the world but was made manifest at the end of the times for your sake" (I Peter 1:20).

Sometimes the Scriptures relate the redemptive purpose of God in Christ not only to the death and resurrection of Jesus but also to the incarnation, apart from which the death of Jesus would have had no redemptive significance. God sent his Son in the likeness of sinful flesh, and for sin condemned sin in the flesh (Rom. 8:3). In the fullness of time God sent forth his Son to redeem us from the law and make us sons of God (Gal. 4:4-6). In this passage there is no specific mention of the death of Christ, though of course it is understood (cf. Gal. 3:13). The Son of God is God's gift to the world (John 3:16). In short, "the Father has sent his Son as the Savior of the world" (I John 4:14).

Jesus was deeply conscious of a divine purpose in the giving of his life. He spoke of his death as a "baptism to be baptized with" (Luke 12:50; cf. Mark 10:39) and as "the cup which the Father has given me" (John 18:11; cf. Mark 10:39; 14:36). "And he began to teach them that the Son of man must suffer . . ." (Mark 8:31), the Greek verb *dei* conveying the idea of "divine necessity."[63] Jesus' sense of acting according to a divine purpose which would meet its culmination by his death in Jerusalem is expressed in his answer to the Pharisees when they warned him to flee because Herod Antipas was seeking to put him to death (Luke 13:31-33). In the Gospel of John Jesus' sense of divine purpose in relation to his death, resurrection, and exaltation is expressed in references to lifting up the Son of Man (John 3:14; 8:28; 12:32-33), "my hour" or "my time" (John 2:4; 7:6, 8, 30; 8:20; 12:23, 27; 13:1; 17:1), and his laying down his life and taking it up again (John 10:17-18).

The atonement has its origin in the love of God or the grace

63 A. M. Hunter, *The Message of the New Testament* (Philadelphia: Westminster Press, 1944), p. 99.

of God. It is "by the grace of God" that Jesus tastes of death for every man (Heb. 2:9). The death of Christ is the supreme manifestation of God's love. "But God shows his love for us in that while we were yet sinners Christ died for us" (Rom. 5:8). The death of Christ on man's behalf is a revelation of God's love because it is God's gift. He "did not spare his own Son but gave him up for us all . . ." (Rom. 8:32). God put forth Christ as an expiation by his blood (Rom. 3:25). In the Johannine literature the revelation of the love of God consists not only in the death of Christ but also in the incarnation which is its presupposition (I John 4:9-10; John 3:16).

V. THE PURPOSE OF THE ATONEMENT

The purpose of the atonement according to the New Testament, stated in the broadest terms, is to deal effectively with our sins in such a way as to deliver us from the penalty, power, and presence of sin, to reconcile us to God, and to bring moral and spiritual renewal by imparting a new principle of life and righteousness.

It is the sin of man that necessitates the atonement, and the sin of man is the problem with which the atonement is intended to deal. Christ's death was a "sacrifice for sins" (Heb. 10:12). Christ "gave himself for our sins . . ." (Gal. 1:4). He was "put to death for our trespasses . . ." (Rom. 4:25). "For Christ also died for our sins once for all . . ." (I Pet. 3:18). "Christ died for our sins in accordance with the scriptures . . ." (I Cor. 15:3). The exact meaning of statements like these is difficult to determine. They may mean: (1) that our sins were responsible for his death, (2) that he bore the responsibilities of our sins or submitted to God's judgment upon our sins, or (3) that he died in order to deliver us from our sins; or they may mean a combination of any or all of these three meanings.

Redemption or deliverance is sometimes represented as the purpose of the atonement. Defined with reference to sin, redemption is primarily forgiveness (Eph. 1:7; Col. 1:14; Matt. 26:28; Luke 24:47; Acts 2:38; 3:18-19; 5:31; 10:43), deliverance (Titus 2:14), putting away sin (Heb. 9:26), taking away sin (John 1:29), bearing sin (Heb. 9:28; I Pet. 2:24), purification for sin (Heb. 1:3), cleansing from sin (I John 1:7) and expiation for sin (Rom. 3:25; Heb. 2:17; I John 2:2). Defined with reference to the Satanic powers which instigate sin, redemption is victory over the evil powers, breaking down their bondage, and the deliverance from their clutches (John 12:31-33; Col. 2:14-15; Heb. 2:14-15; cf. I Cor. 2:8; Gal. 1:4). Defined with reference to the law, it is the deliverance from a system in which salvation is sought on the basis of human merit as judged by legal demands (Gal. 3:12-14; Col. 2:13-14; Gal. 5:1; Eph. 2:8-9; Rom. 7-8). Defined with reference to death, redemption is the deliverance from the fear of death (Heb. 2:15). This deliverance comes on the basis of the confidence in an eternal redemption wrought by Christ (Heb. 9:12) and in the knowledge that through Christ we have passed from death into life (John 5:24; 3:15-16; 6:51, 53-58; 10:27-28; 17:3).

The New Testament often views the purpose of the atonement in terms of reconciliation. "For Christ also died for sins once for all, the righteous for the unrighteous, that he might bring us to God . . ." (I Pet. 3:18). "God was in Christ reconciling the world to himself . . ." (II Cor. 5:19). The cross acts as a magnetic force in drawing men to Christ (John 12: 32-33). ". . . While we were enemies we were reconciled to God by the death of his Son" (Rom. 5:10). Peace with God (Rom. 5:1) and access to God (Rom. 5:2; Eph. 2:18; Heb. 4: 14-16; 10:19-22) are among the blessings attending reconciliation. Reconciliation is first of all reconciliation to God; but Paul speaks also of the reconciliation of Jews and Gentiles through the cross (Eph. 2:18), and he hints at the cosmic dimensions of reconciliation (Col. 1:20).

A permanent standing with God defined in terms of justification and sonship is also among the benefits of the atonement, and thus doubtless one of the purposes for which it was effected (Rom. 3:24-25; 4:25; 5:9, 16, 18). The writer of Hebrews speaks of the purpose of Christ's death or that which is achieved through it in terms of sanctification (Heb. 2:11; 10:10, 14; 13:12), but the meaning which he attaches to sanctification in such passages seems to be the same as that which Paul gives to justification.[64]

Again, the purpose of the death of Christ is sometimes expressed in terms of the establishment of a new covenant. That Jesus so interpreted his death is obvious from his words about the blood of the covenant in connection with the institution of the Lord's Supper (I Cor. 11:25; Matt. 26:28; Mark 14:24;

[64] Denny, *op. cit.*, p. 126.

cf. Jer. 31:31-34). Matthew 26:28 speaks specifically of blood "poured out for many for the forgiveness of sins," thus defining the meaning of the covenant in terms of Jeremiah 31:34. The writer of Hebrews speaks of Christ as "the mediator of a new covenant" (Heb. 9:15), and he interprets Jeremiah's promise concerning the establishment of a new covenant as fulfilled in the sacrifice of Christ (Heb. 8:6-13; cf. Jer. 31:31-34). He also recognizes that the new covenant, unlike the old one, is an "eternal covenant" (Heb. 13:20). Closely connected with the new covenant idea is that of Christ ransoming for himself "a people of his own who are zealous for good deeds" (Titus 2:14; I Pet. 2:9-10; Mark 10:45; I Cor. 6:20; I Tim. 2:5-6).

The atonement is also designed to bring moral and spiritual renewal. Christ "bore our sins in his own body on the tree, that we might die to sin and live to righteousness" (I Pet. 2:24). His sacrifice has the power of purifying the "conscience from dead works to serve the living God" (Heb. 9:14). "And he died for all, that those who live might live no longer for themselves but for him who for their sake died and was raised" (II Cor. 5:15). Christ "died for us that whether we wake or sleep we might live with him" (I Thess. 5:10; cf. II Cor. 4:10; Rom. 14:9). Christ "condemned sin in the flesh, in order that the just requirements of the law might be fulfilled in us, who walk not according to the flesh but according to the Spirit" (Rom. 8: 3-4). Christ "gave himself for us to redeem us from all iniquity and to purify for himself a people of his own who are zealous for good deeds" (Titus 2:14). When by baptism we participate in Christ's death and resurrection we arise to "walk in newness of life" (Rom. 6:4).

VI. Categories for Interpreting the Atonement

1. *Vicarious Atonement.* To say that Christ's death is vicarious is to say that he died for others or with their benefit in view. Christ died for me (Gal. 2:20), for you (Heb. 9:14), for us (Rom. 5:8; Eph. 5:2; I Thess. 5:10; I Pet. 2:21, 24; 3:18; I John 3:16), for us all (Rom. 8:32), for the sheep (John 10:11, 15), for the church (Eph. 5:25), for his friends (John 15:13), for the ungodly (Rom. 5:6), for the people (John 11:50; 18: 14), for many (Mark 10:45), for every one (Heb. 2:9), for all (II Cor. 5:14; I Tim. 2:6). The category of vicarious atonement is an all-inclusive one. Because of its breadth, however,

it is ambiguous. It neither defines the sense in which Christ died for man, nor explains the logical connection between the death of Christ and the benefits secured by his death.

2. *Sacrificial Atonement.* "The sacrificial aspect of the Atonement," says Taylor, "is one of the most widely attested ideas in New Testament teaching."[65] Indeed, sacrificial ideas pervade every segment of the New Testament. Taylor reminds us that references to the "blood" of Christ are three times as numerous as those to "the death" of Christ.[66] Taylor thinks that the followers of Jesus with such expressions as "the blood of Christ" sought to find the deeper meaning in the Old Testament cultus of sacrifice which was fulfilled in the sacrifice of Christ. Self-giving and complete dedication to God are among the connotations of the term "the blood of Christ," but they are not the only ones. Included in the list of derivative ideas is "the thought of life through death and an offering through which men may draw nigh to God."[67]

Four sacrificial terms are found in the words which Jesus used in the institution of the Lord's Supper (I Cor. 11:23ff.; Mark 14: 22ff.) : "blood" (Lev. 17:11), "covenant" (Ex. 24:8), "poured out" (Lev. 4:7, 8), and "body."[68] We have already seen that Jesus interpreted his mission in terms of the fulfilment of the spiritualized concept of sacrifice found in Isaiah 53, and that the influence of the Servant conception as found in the Servant Songs of Deutero-Isaiah is echoed throughout the New Testament.

The writer of Hebrews obviously regards the category of sacrifice as the key for the interpretation of the atonement. If we tried to substantiate this claim by quotations from the epistle, it would be difficult to know where to begin or end; for the central theme of this epistle is that Christ is an eternal high priest after the order of Melchizedek, who by offering himself once-for-all as the perfect sacrifice for sin does what the Old Testament sacrifices could never do and secures eternal redemption. The Old Testament sacrifices are of value, however, in that they foreshadow the perfect sacrifice made by Christ (Heb. 10:1).

---

65 Taylor, *The Atonement in New Testament Teaching,* p. 177.
66 *Loc. cit.*
67 *Ibid.,* p. 25.
68 Hunter, *op. cit.,* p. 107.

No other New Testament writer makes such an extensive use of the category of sacrifice, but sacrificial ideas pervade the teachings of the epistles of Paul, I Peter, and the Johannine literature. Paul calls Christ "our paschal lamb" (I Cor. 5:7), and a similar idea is expressed in I Peter 1:18-19 in the words: "You know that you were ransomed . . . not with perishable things such as silver or gold, but with the precious blood of Christ, like that of a lamb without blemish or spot."

Sacrificial ideas are evident in Paul's admonition: "And walk in love, as Christ loved us and gave himself up for us, a fragrant offering and sacrifice to God" (Eph. 5:2). But the clearest statement of a sacrificial interpretation of the death of Christ in the epistles of Paul is the declaration that God has put forth Christ Jesus "as an expiation by his blood, to be received by faith" (Rom. 3:25). The sacrifice has its origin in the grace of God (Rom. 3:24), for it is God who puts it forward. The mention of "expiation" (*hilasterion*) and "blood" in the same passage makes the sacrificial significance unmistakable. The words "to be received by faith" indicate what is the case with any true interpretation of sacrificial worship, that is, that it requires the response of the worshipper to be effective. "The Greek word (*hilasterion*)," says C. H. Dodd,

> is derived from a verb which in pagan writers and inscriptions has two meanings: (a) 'to placate' a man or a god; (b) 'to expiate' a sin, i.e. to perform an act (such as the payment of a fine or the offering of a sacrifice) by which its guilt is annulled. The former meaning is overwhelmingly the more common. In the Septuagint, on the other hand, the meaning (a) is practically unknown where God is the object, and the meaning (b) is found in scores of passages. Thus the biblical sense of the verb is 'to perform an act whereby guilt or defilement is removed.'[69]

Since it is God who sets forth Christ Jesus as the *hilasterion*, the meaning in Romans 3:25 is not that of propitiating an angry deity but of covering sin or annulling its guilt. It may thus be translated "expiation" or "atoning sacrifice." By setting forth Christ as an atoning sacrifice God demonstrated his righteousness in providing a way of salvation for man by judging his sin (Rom. 3:26).

69 C. H. Dodd, *The Epistle of Paul to the Romans* (New York: Harper and Row, 1932), p. 54.

The verb *hilasakesthai* occurs in Hebrews 2:17 and the noun *hilasmos* in I John 2:2 and 4:10. The idea of expiation or an atoning sacrifice is clear in all of these references. There is no idea of placating an angry deity in any of these passages. This is particularly clear, however, in I John 4:10: "In this is love, not that we loved God but that he loved us and sent his Son to be the expiation for our sins."

The scapegoat idea probably underlies John 1:29 and I John 3:5. Sacrificial overtones are evident, also, in passages which speak of cleansing through the blood of Christ (e.g., I John 1:7; Rev. 7:14) and redemption through his blood (e.g., Rev. 1:5; 5:9).

3. *Representative Atonement and Substitutionary Atonement.* The category of representative atonement means that, in the saving work of Christ which reached its climax with the death and resurrection of Jesus, Christ did something for the salvation of sinful men, acting on their behalf as their representative. The New Testament concept of representative atonement is based on the Old Testament concept of corporate personality. Both the Son of Man and the Suffering Servant in both Old Testament prophecy and the New Testament fulfilment are representative figures. Surely the idea of representation is found in the words of Jesus concerning the giving of his life as a ransom for many (Mark 10:45) and the blood of the covenant which is poured out for many (Mark 14:24).

Paul interprets Christ as the constitutor and head of a new humanity, the second Adam who regains for man all that was lost in the first Adam. The human race is thus regarded as summed up in its two representatives, Adam and Christ, by whom the religious histories of all descended from them are determined.

> Then as one man's trespass led to condemnation for all men, so one man's act of righteousness leads to acquittal and life for all men. For as by one man's disobedience many were made sinners, so by one man's obedience many will be made righteous (Rom. 5:18-19; cf. Rom. 5:12-21; I Cor. 15:21-22, 45-50).

Paul says, ". . . the love of Christ controls us" (the love which is manifested in the death of Christ) because we interpret the death of Christ to mean "that one has died for all; therefore all have died" (II Cor. 5:14). Christ died for all; and since he is the representative of the whole race, all died in him. "And he died for all, that those who live might no longer live for themselves but for him who for their sake died and was raised" (II Cor. 5:15).

Closely associated with the idea of Christ as the constitutor of a new humanity is that of Christ as the mighty warrior who wins a decisive victory over all of the evil powers that hold man in bondage: sin, death, the devil, the law, and the wrath of God (John 8:34; Rom. 6:16; I Cor. 15:20, 54-57; John 12: 31-33; I Cor. 2:8; Col. 2:14-15; Heb. 2:14-15; Gal. 3:13; Rom. 5: 9). The victory which he won he won as our representative, and we participate in this victory by faith.

The central concept of the Epistle to the Hebrews — that of Christ as our high priest who once-for-all makes the perfect sacrifice for sin and secures eternal redemption, who as our high priest ever lives to make intercession for us — is a representative concept. The same is true of the idea expressed in I Timothy 2:5-6 of Christ as the one Mediator between God and man, who gave himself as a ransom for all.

But is the atonement to be regarded as substitutionary as well as representative? Taylor rejects the idea because he thinks that to admit the substitutionary element in the death of Christ would be to open the door for many false assumptions commonly associated with the penal substitution theory; namely, that there is a transfer of guilt from the sinner to the Saviour, that the Father and the Son are divided in the atonement, and that the atonement works automatically apart from faith-union with Christ which results in newness of life.[70] While rejecting all of these false assumptions, we may still speak of a substitutionary element in the death of Christ.

Passages like II Corinthians 5:21; Galatians 3:13; I Peter 2: 24 and 3:18 may be subsumed under the category of representative atonement as is the case in Taylor's treatment of them, but they more naturally fall into the category of substitutionary atonement. Christ's action on behalf of man easily becomes action in man's stead. A clear example of this is I Peter 3:18: "For Christ also died for sins once for all, the righteous for the unrighteous, that he might bring us to God." Though the preposition *huper*, "on behalf of," is used in this passage the resultant idea is clearly this: the unrighteous should have

---

[70] Taylor, *The Atonement in New Testament Teaching*, pp. 174-76.

died, but the righteous died in their place. I Peter 2:24 means
that Jesus took upon himself the responsibility for our sins (cf.
Isa. 53:5-6). This is probably not to be interpreted in any
legalistic sense which would regard guilt as having been transferred from the sinner to the Saviour. Rather it means that Jesus
so identified himself with us in our sins that the penalty for sin
which should have fallen upon us fell upon him. The same is
true of II Corinthians 5:21 and Galatians 3:13, and possibly
of Mark 10:45, where *anti,* the preposition normally meaning
"instead of," is used. The atonement is effected and salvation
is completed by means of a two-way identification: Christ identifies himself with us in our sin; by faith we identify ourselves
with him in his righteousness and become united to him. "Thereby His attitude to sin becomes our attitude, His love for the
Father our love, His passion for holiness our passion."[71]

Though Christ died for sins once-for-all, and in this sense
his atoning work is a finished work, nevertheless it becomes
effective for us and we receive its benefits only as by faith we are
united with Christ in death and resurrection, dying to sin and
rising to newness of life in Christ (Rom. 3:25-26; 5:1; Acts 16:
31; Gal. 2:19-20; Luke 9:23; I Pet. 2:21-25). Both the saving
work of Christ in his death and resurrection and our appropriation of it are symbolized in the ordinances, baptism and the
Lord's Supper.

[71] James Stewart, *A Man in Christ* (New York: Harper and Row),
p. 241.

Chapter Three

Historical Interpretations of the Atonement

In a discussion like this, which aims at brevity and simplicity, it is impossible to avoid the impression of arbitrariness in the selection of the men to be discussed and the distortion which comes from oversimplification in the manner in which their theological ideas are treated. The selection of men has been made on the basis of the writer's evaluation of the originality and influence of their ideas; and the discussion of their theories is presented with the idea of indicating the salient features of their interpretations of the atonement, rather than a complete summary of their theological systems. The historical course of development supplies the framework within which the various theories are treated, though within this basic framework some attempt is made to classify theologians according to the general theological positions which they represent.

I. The First Thousand Years

1. *The Dominant Theme.* The dominant theme is that of victory, the deliverance of man from the evil powers which hold him in bondage. Because this victory is usually treated as accomplished through a ransom to the devil, the theory is frequently designated "the ransom theory." In one form or another it was so widely held by the early church fathers that it is

often called "the patristic theory." Since among the church
fathers this kind of view was more widely held in the Eastern
Church than in the Western Church, this view is often designated as the "Eastern" or "Greek" view in distinction from the
"Western" or "Latin" type, later more fully developed by Anselm.
Gustav Aulén, who is the leading advocate of this kind of interpretation among modern theologians, has applied three other
names to it, which have been accepted rather generally.[1] He
calls it "the classic view" because of his conviction that it is the
oldest and truest theory of the saving work of Christ. He calls
it "dramatic" because he claims that it views the atonement in
terms of dramatic struggle, conflict, and victory. He also des-
ignates it as "Christus Victor" because of the emphasis upon the
victory of Christ over the evil powers.

Aulén starts with Irenaeus (ca. 130-200 A.D.) in his treatment of the Christus Victor theme. He treats this theme as the
integrating center for all of Irenaeus' theology concerning the
work of Christ. This is probably an oversimplification which
does not do full justice to the themes of incarnation and re-
capitulation in Irenaeus' theology. Nevertheless, the Christus
Victor theme is clearly an important part of Irenaeus' theological standpoint. ". . . He (Christ) bound the strong man, and
set free the weak, and endowed His own handiwork with salvation, by destroying sin."[2]

> For the Lord, through means of suffering, 'ascending into the
> lofty place, led captivity captive, gave gifts to men' . . . Our
> Lord also by His passion destroyed death, and dispersed error,
> and put an end of corruption, and destroyed ignorance, while
> He manifested life and revealed truth, and bestowed the gift
> of incorruption.[3]

And though the devil had gained dominion over us unjustly,
snatching us away from the omnipotent God to whom we by
nature belonged, God did not use violence to gain back that

---

[1] Gustav Aulén, *Christus Victor*, American edition (New York: The Macmillan Company, 1951).

[2] Irenaeus, "Against Heresies," III, XVIII, 6, *The Ante-Nicene Fathers*,
Alexander Roberts and James Donaldson, editors (Buffalo: The Christian
Literature Publishing Company, 1885), Vol. I. Hereafter, quotations from
The Ante-Nicene Fathers will be designated *ANF*.

[3] "Against Heresies," II, XX, 3, *ANF*, Vol. I.

which rightly belonged to him, but used persuasion, dealing justly even with the unjust, and gave the Word as a ransom.[4] Robert S. Paul summarizes as follows:

> This aspect of Irenaeus' 'theory' of the Atonement contains three related ideas. First, that Man is in bondage through sin to the Devil as a real and authoritative power; secondly, that in order to effect his release man must be bought back by a ransom to which the Devil would consent; and thirdly, that this redemption depends entirely upon the nature of God, upon a justice that would give even the Devil his due, and upon the merciful love that showed itself in readiness to intervene on Man's behalf.[5]

Aulén claims that "the classic idea" of the atonement "dominates the whole of Greek patristic theology from Irenaeus to John of Damascus," [6] the basic idea being set forth, with a diversity of expressions, in the works of Origen, Athanasius, Basil the Great, Gregory of Nyssa, Gregory of Nazianzus, Cyril of Alexandria, Cyril of Jerusalem, and Chrysostom. While recognizing that the Western Fathers were influenced somewhat by ideas of the Latin type, Aulén[7] nevertheless maintains that "the classic idea" was the dominant view among the Western Fathers as well, being found in Ambrose, Pseudo-Ambrose, Augustine, Leo the Great, Caesarius of Arles, Faustus of Rhegium, and Gregory the Great. Again Aulén has probably overstated his case, but he is doubtless right that "the classic view" in some form or other is found in the writings of all the above-named theologians.

Origen (ca. 185-254 A.D.) raises the question as to whom the ransom was paid, and denies that it was paid to God, affirming that it was paid to the devil.[8] Hastings Rashdall argues that in Origen the ransom is a metaphor taken from the battlefield. It is a "ransom paid to a conqueror who has physically carried off a prisoner."[9] "That the ransom was paid to the Devil merely

---

[4] *Ibid.,* V, I, 1.

[5] Robert S. Paul, *The Atonement and the Sacraments* (London: Hodder and Stoughton, 1961), p. 53.

[6] Aulén, *op. cit.,* p. 37.

[7] *Ibid.,* p. 39.

[8] "Commentary on Matthew," XVI, 8; cf. *The Early Christian Fathers,* edited and translated by Henry Bettenson (London: Oxford University Press, 1956).

[9] Hastings Rashdall, *The Idea of Atonement in Christian Theology* (London: Macmillan and Co., 1925), pp. 260-61.

means that the Devil did actually succeed in bringing about Christ's death."[10] Origen introduces the idea that the devil was deceived into an action which brought about his own ruin. Fearing that the human race would be delivered from his grasp by Christ's teachings, the devil instigated the crucifixion of Jesus, not knowing that the efficacy of Christ's death would exceed that of his teaching and miracles.[11]

To Origen it was Christ's resurrection on the third day that turned Christ's death into victory over death and him who has the power of death, the devil.[12]

Gregory of Nyssa (ca. 335-395 A.D.) affirms that the devil had a just claim over man, since through the fall man had voluntarily placed himself under the devil's power. Like Irenaeus, Gregory of Nyssa asserts that God would use no violence in redeeming man from the devil; for had he done so, man would not have been rightfully redeemed. To redeem man God paid the devil, man's owner, all that he asked as the redemption price for his property. The devil, being dazzled by Christ's miracles, recognized in Christ a bargain greater than that which he had, and "chose him as the ransom for those whom he had shut up in death's prison."[13] But the devil was deceived because the deity of Christ was veiled in flesh. In a grotesque figure of speech Gregory compares the devil to a greedy fish who is caught on the hook of Christ's deity when he is enticed to swallow it by the bait of Christ's flesh.[14] Gregory raises the question as to whether it was legitimate for God to deceive the devil. He concludes that it was both just and good. It was just because the deceiver reaped what he sowed, being himself deceived. It was good also because in it God had a good purpose, which was the redemption of the devil along with man. "For when death came into contact with life, darkness with light, corruption with incorruption, the worse of these things disappeared

10 *Loc. cit.*

11 *Ibid.*, p. 262.

12 Origen, "Commentary on Matthew," XIII, 9, *ANF*, Vol. IX, p. 480.

13 Gregory of Nyssa, "An Address on Religious Instruction," Chapter 23. Translation and text found in *The Library of Christian Classics*, Vol. III, *The Christology of the Later Fathers* (Philadelphia: Westminster Press, first published, MCMLIV). Hereafter *The Library of Christian Classics* will be referred to as *LCC*.

14 *Ibid.*, Chapter 24.

into a state of nonexistence, to the profit of him who was freed from these evils."[15]

Gregory of Nazianzus (ca. 330-90 A.D.) rejected the idea that a ransom was paid to the devil or to God. Rather, he sought to explain the atonement under the category of sacrifice.

Augustine, like Gregory of Nyssa, recognized the devil's just claim on man. God justly committed man to the power of the devil when Adam sinned. But the devil exceeded his rights when he shed innocent blood in slaying Christ. Therefore, "it was no more than justice that he should deliver up those that were in bondage to him."[16] Whereas Gregory of Nyssa had used the figure of a fishhook, Augustine used the figure of a mousetrap. "What did our redeemer do to our captor? As our price, He held out His cross as a mousetrap and set as bait upon it His own blood."[17]

How are we to evaluate the ransom theory? Such grotesque imagery as the fishhook and the mousetrap, employed by Gregory of Nyssa and Augustine, respectively, are certainly repulsive to modern man. After all, the biblical term "ransom" (*lutron* or *antilutron*) is probably only a figure of speech indicating that our redemption is costly. We use a similar expression sometimes when we say that a mother pays a big price when she brings a child into the world. But it would be absurd to ask to whom the mother pays the price. Even so, it is meaningless to ask to whom the ransom is paid that effects our redemption. Nevertheless, the Christus Victor theme, the idea that Christ through his incarnation, life, death and resurrection wins a decisive victory over all the evil powers which hold man in bondage — sin, death, and the devil — is certainly biblical. And Aulén has made us all indebted to him by revitalizing this biblical theme for our day. We shall return to this idea when we attempt a constructive statement of the meaning of atonement.

2. *Subordinate Themes.* Redemption by incarnation and redemption by penal sacrifice are two other themes expressed again and again during the first thousand years of Christian theology.

Rightly understood, the incarnation is the presupposition of

15 *Ibid.,* Ch. 26.

16 Paul, *op. cit.,* p. 60.

17 Augustine, Sermon CXXX, 2; quoted by Sydney Cave, *The Doctrine of the Work of Christ* (London: Hodder and Stoughton, first printed, 1937, fifth impression, 1959), p. 119.

the atonement; but at times the subject is so treated as to give
the impression that it is the incarnation itself, Christ's union
with the race, which effects redemption. Sometimes called the
"physical" theory or "mystical" theory, this type of view suggests that "human nature was sanctified, transformed and ele-
vated by the very act of Christ's becoming man."[18] Some typi-
cal statements are as follows:

> Our Lord Jesus Christ . . . did, through His transcendent love,
> become what we are, that He might bring us to be even what He
> is Himself.[19]
>
> God lived on man's level, that man might be able to live on
> God's level: God was found weak that man might become most
> great.[20]
>
> For this he came down, for this he assumed human nature, for
> this he willingly endured the sufferings of man, that by being
> reduced to the measure of our weakness he might raise us to
> the measure of his power.[21]
>
> The Word . . . became man just that you may learn from a
> man how it may be that man should become God.[22]
>
> For he was made man that we might be made God; and he mani-
> fested himself by a body that we might receive the idea of the
> unseen Father; and he endured the insolence of men that we
> might inherit immortality.[23]

In these statements, not only is the incarnation set forth as the
means of salvation, but also salvation is expressed in terms of
the deification of human nature. This sounds like self-idolatry,
but probably Wolf is right when he explains that in its context
it does not mean that men cease to be creatures and become
gods. Rather it is the way the fathers had of describing salvation
as "advance to new status," of indicating that God's purpose
for man is not simple restoration but cure and new life.[24]

[18] J. N. D. Kelly, *Early Christian Doctrines* (London: Adam & Charles
Black, 1958) , p. 375.

[19] Irenaeus, "Against Heresies," Book V, Preface, *ANF*, Vol. I, p. 526.

[20] Tertullian, "Adversus Marcionem," ii, 27; translated by Bettenson,
op. cit., p. 168.

[21] Clement of Alexandria, "Quis Dives Salvetur," 37; translated by
Bettenson, *op. cit.*, p. 240.

[22] Clement of Alexandria, "Protrepticus," i, 8, 4; translated by Bettenson,
op. cit., p. 244.

[23] Athanasius, "On the Incarnation," 54, *LCC*, Vol. III, pp. 107-08.

[24] William J. Wolf, *No Cross, No Crown* (Garden City: Doubleday &
Company, 1957) , p. 97.

The patristic writers also represented salvation as the restoration of the divine image in man, and deliverance from the power of death and corruption, the former emphasis being particularly strong in Irenaeus and the latter in Athanasius.

Irenaeus laid great stress upon Paul's doctrine of Christ as the second Adam through whom we recover all that was lost in the first Adam. As many were made sinners through the disobedience of Adam, so many are made righteous through the obedience of Christ.[25] The basic premise of both Paul and Irenaeus is that "if we fell through our solidarity with the first man, we can be restored through our solidarity with Christ."[26] This idea of Christ as the representative man is, according to Kelly, "one grand theme" in almost all the patristic attempts to explain redemption, and the theme which "provides the clue to the fathers' understanding of the work of Christ."[27]

The so-called Latin view of the atonement, later expounded more fully by Anselm, and in a somewhat different form by Luther and Calvin, had its precursors among the church fathers. Though this type of interpretation is more generally associated with the Western Fathers than the Eastern Fathers, it is found in both. Kelly goes so far as to call it "the main stream of Greek soteriology in the fourth century."[28] Among the church fathers of East and West whose writings, at least in part, express in various ways the idea of Christ propitiating the Father by paying the penalty of man's sins through his death are the following: Tertullian, Cyprian, Origen, Athanasius, Gregory of Nyssa, Eusebius of Caesarea, Cyril of Jerusalem, Basil, Gregory of Nazianzus, John Chrysostom, Hilary, Ambrose, Augustine, Theodore of Mopsuestia, and Theodoret.[29]

Origen's interpretation of the atonement is many-sided, but one of his distinct emphases is that Christ "has taken our sins upon Himself, has borne them and suffered freely for us," that he has propitiated the Father by offering himself as a spotless sacrifice.[30] Augustine, by attributing the mediatorial activity of Christ to his existence as man and not as the Word, helped pave the way for the Latin interpretation which made it appear

25 Cf. "Against Heresies," III, XVIII, 7.
26 *Op. cit.*, p. 172.
27 Kelly, *op. cit.*, p. 376.
28 *Ibid.*, p. 384.
29 Cf. Kelly, *op. cit.*, pp. 186, 375-99.
30 *Ibid.*, p. 186.

that God and Christ were divided in the atonement.[31] Gregory
of Nyssa and Theodoret, among others, applied Isaiah 53 to
Christ and interpreted the death of Christ in terms of Christ
as our substitute accepting the penalty which was due to us
because of our sins.[32]

Tertullian used both the words "satisfaction" and "merit,"
but he defined them in terms of penance. Defining penance
as the compensation which a man makes for his fault, he maintained that penance is satisfaction. Tertullian defined merit
in terms of the performance of what is commanded, the observ-
ance of law. Since some acts such as fasting, voluntary celibacy,
and martyrdom are beyond the call of duty, one can obtain excess merit by performing them. Tertullian had nothing to say
about the transfer of excess merit from one person to another.
This idea was developed by Cyprian, who maintained that
Christ by his suffering and death had earned an excess of merit,
which is paid to God as satisfaction, and which is transferable
to man's account. Gregory the Great applied these ideas to sacrifice. The sin of man demands a sacrifice, but no animal sacrifice is sufficient. A human sacrifice is required. But the sacrifice must be undefiled. Since no one who is born of sinful
seed is sinless, the Son of God was born of a virgin, and took
upon himself human nature, apart from sin, and made the
sacrifice on man's behalf.[33] Thus the stage was set for Anselm.

From the above discussion it should be evident that the
church fathers of the first millennium of the Christian era interpreted the saving work of Christ from various points of view,
the varying interpretations sometimes being found in the same
authors and in the closest proximity to each other. Though
the Christus Victor theme may be designated as the dominant
theme, distortion is introduced into the picture unless it is recognized that other ideas also find frequent and forceful expression.

The fact of the matter is that during the first few centuries
of the Christian era the church was concerned mainly about
such doctrines as the incarnation of the Word, the relation
of the human and divine elements in Christ, and the doctrine of
the Trinity. How Christ saves us never became a subject of

31 Cave, *op. cit.,* p. 122.
32 Kelly, *op. cit.,* pp. 382, 395.
33 Cf. Aulén, *op. cit.,* pp. 81-84.

controversy, and so it never received major attention. The church fathers, however, could hardly be said to have been indifferent to the doctrine of the atonement. Athanasius' great concern for preserving a true interpretation of the person of Christ was rooted in the conviction that if Christ is not one *(homoousios,* of the same substance) with the Father, he cannot save. Nevertheless, it is true that no attempt at an elaborate treatment or a definitive statement of a rationale of atonement was made until Anselm.

II. Anselm: The Satisfaction Theory

It was Anselm (1033-1109 A.D.) who, in *Cur Deus Homo?* (1098), placed the atonement in the limelight of theological consideration. Adolph Harnack calls Anselm the first theologian to frame "a *theory,* both of the necessity of the appearing of the God-man, and of the necessity of His death."[34] Cave speaks of Anselm's book as "a theological classic the influence of which it would be difficult to exaggerate."[35] J. K. Mozley says:

> If any one Christian work, outside the canon of the New Testament, may be described as 'epoch-making,' it is the *Cur Deus Homo* of Anselm. It has affected, though in different degrees, and by way now of attraction, now of repulsion, all soteriological thought since his time.[36]

Anselm attempts, apart from the facts of the atonement as revealed in the Scriptures and relying solely upon reason, to give a demonstration of the necessity of the incarnation and the atonement in Christ which will be convincing for Jews, Mohammedans, and pagans alike. His argument is set forth in the form of a dialogue between Anselm and his pupil, Boso, in which Boso raises the questions frequently posed by unbelievers and Anselm answers them. Anselm's book is divided into two parts, the first showing that it is impossible for any man to be saved apart from Christ, and the second showing that salvation has been provided through Christ, the God-man.

The basic question which Boso poses and which Anselm seeks

---

[34] Adolph Harnack, *History of Dogma,* translated from the third German edition by Neil Buchanan (Boston: Little, Brown, and Company, 1899), Vol. VI, p. 56.

[35] Cave, *op. cit.,* p. 130.

[36] J. K. Mozley, *The Doctrine of the Atonement* (London: Duckworth, first published in 1915, 1947 reprint), p. 125.

to answer is that which relates to the necessity and reason which
"led God, although he is almighty, to take upon him the lowli-
ness and weakness of human nature in order to renew it."[37]
Though Anselm seeks to establish his argument on the basis
of reason apart from the knowledge of Christ which comes by
revelation, his argument is not devoid of presuppositions which
are based on scriptural teachings. One of these is the fall of
man and the solidarity of the human race in sin. Because of
the fall, the human race was altogether ruined; and God's plan
for man was about to become of no effect. In Anselm's thinking
the necessity of the incarnation and the atonement rests upon
the presupposition that it was not fitting for God's plan for man
to be entirely wiped out, but that this plan could be put into
effect only if the human race were delivered by its Creator
himself.[38] If man's redemption had been effected by a man
or an angel or any being who was not God, man would not have
been restored to his former dignity; for this would mean that
he who was created to be the servant of God alone would become the servant of a being who is not God.[39]

Anselm uses his pupil, Boso, to attack the idea in patristic
theology that through the fall Satan had obtained just rights
over man and that the atonement is a ransom paid to the
devil. While recognizing that man is justly subject to the ill-
treatment of the devil, and that God justly allows this, Boso
maintains, nevertheless, that it is unjust for the devil to torment
man, since he himself is a rebellious servant of God. God uses
the devil, however, to show man that since he has freely sinned,
it is impossible for him to avoid sin or the penalty of sin.[40] The
point that Anselm is making through Boso is that the ransom
was not paid to the devil. Anselm devotes the rest of his book
to demonstrating that the ransom was both required by God
and paid by God. He uses the term "satisfaction," however,
instead of "ransom."

Maintaining that the forgiveness of sins is necessary for man
if he is to arrive at blessedness, Anselm proceeds to show what

[37] "Why God Became Man," I, 1, LCC, Vol. X, A Scholastic Miscellany:
Anselm to Ockham, edited and translated by Eugene R. Fairweather (London: SCM Press, 1956). Quotations from Anselm are all from Fairweather's
translation.
[38] Ibid., I, 4.
[39] Ibid., I, 5.
[40] Ibid., I, 7.

it means to sin and to make satisfaction for sins. He defines sin as failing to render to God his due. What man owes to God is to make every inclination subject to the will of God. "One who does not render this honor to God takes away from God what belongs to him, and dishonors God, and to do this is to sin."[41] It is not enough for man simply to return to God that which he has taken away. In view of the insult and dishonor which he has brought to God, he must give back more than he has taken away; that is, he must make satisfaction for his sin. If due satisfaction for sin is not made, the only way God can deal rightly with sin is to punish it. Thus Anselm poses the alternative, either satisfaction or punishment. But if God punished the sin of man in man, he would completely destroy his handiwork, and thus bring to nought his purpose in creation. Thus satisfaction must be made for man's sin.

But man cannot make satisfaction for his own sins for two reasons. The first reason is that he already owes God complete obedience; he has nothing to pay God as "satisfaction" that he does not already owe, even if a satisfaction were unnecessary. The second reason that man cannot make satisfaction for his own sins is that sin takes on the quality of infinity because it is committed against the infinite God. There is no more famous sentence in the whole book than Anselm's words to Boso, "You have not yet considered what a heavy weight sin is."[42] Sinful man, who has been overcome by the devil, cannot restore to God what is his due unless he overcomes the devil. But this is what he cannot do, since through the wound of sin he is conceived and born in sin.[43] Boso sums up for Anselm, and brings the first part of the book to a conclusion with the observation that "sinful man owes God a debt for sin which he cannot repay, and at the same time that he cannot be saved without repaying it. . . ."[44]

Anselm begins part two by emphasizing again the sublimity of God's purpose for man. God created man for a blessed immortality, but God can complete that which he has begun only by a complete satisfaction for sin. The satisfaction paid to God must be "something greater than everything that exists, except God." "But there is nothing above everything that is not God,

41 *Ibid.,* I, 11.
42 *Ibid.,* I, 21.
43 *Ibid.,* I, 22, 23.
44 *Ibid.,* I, 25.

save God himself."[45] No one but God can make the satisfaction, but no one but man should make it, since it is man who sinned. Thus the satisfaction must be made by a God-man, one who is "both perfect God and perfect man, because none but true God can make it, and none but true man owes it."[46] Thus Anselm has established the necessity of the incarnation. Incarnation is for the purpose of atonement.

Anselm then proceeds to explain, to the satisfaction of his pupil, Boso, that the one who makes satisfaction must be one of Adam's race, since it is man of Adam's race who is in sin; that he must be born of a virgin, and thus free of sin; that the virgin herself is preserved from sin by faith in the death of the one whom she is to bear; and that it was appropriate for the Son to become man, rather than for the Father or the Holy Spirit to do so.[47]

The Son, in his incarnate life, rendered the Father perfect obedience, which, of course, he owed to the Father. But since he had never sinned, and death is the penalty of sin, through his death he accomplished something which has excess merit. Moreover, the merit of this death outweighs all sins, however great they are in magnitude and number. The reason for this is that "no greatness or multitude of sins apart from God's person can be compared to an injury done to the bodily life of this Man."[48] But the merit of the death of the God-man can even wipe out the sins of those who put him to death, since they did it in ignorance. Even Adam and Eve had a share in this redemption.

Last of all, Anselm attempts to show how the death of Christ is paid to God for the sins of man; that is, the connection between Christ's death and man's salvation. In doing so he makes a passing reference to the gentleness and patience of Christ in enduring insults in his death on the cross as an example to men to teach them "not to turn away from the justice they owe to God on account of any trials which they can experience."[49] Moreover, he maintains that the Son in his death offered his humanity to his own divinity as well as to the Father and the Holy Spirit. The heart of Anselm's argument, however,

[45] *Ibid.*, II, 6.
[46] *Ibid.*, II, 7.
[47] *Ibid.*, II, 8, 9.
[48] *Ibid.*, II, 14.
[49] *Ibid.*, II, 18.

is as follows. The Son, through his free gift to the Father, obtained excess merit, which requires a reward from God. Since all that the Father has, however, belongs to the Son and the Son has need of nothing, the reward cannot be paid directly to the Son. Thus the reward is given in the form of salvation to those for whose sake the Son became man. In the incarnation and the death of the Son the great mercy of God as well as the justice of God is demonstrated.

The redemption achieved by Christ, however, is of no avail to the devil. It was necessary for man to be redeemed by a God-man. Fallen angels could be redeemed only by a God-angel. But since the angels are not all descended from one angel, this would be impossible.

The tremendous influence of Anselm's *Cur Deus Homo?* has already been mentioned. Anselm performed a splendid service for theology by bringing the doctrine of the atonement out into the forefront of theological consideration. Hereafter the doctrine of atonement never again could be regarded as of secondary importance. Moreover, by connecting his discussion of the atonement with the problem of the incarnation Anselm built a bridge between what had been the dominant problem of the first millennium of the Christian era to what was to be the dominant problem of the second millennium. By clearly denying the devil's rights over man, he freed the doctrine of the atonement from the grotesque forms of thought in which the patristic doctrine had come to be formulated. As had never been done before, he gave a clear, logical, and understandable explanation both of the necessity of the incarnation and of the death of Christ. Another great merit of Anselm's theory is the seriousness with which it views the problem of sin.

As great as was Anselm's achievement, however, the view which he espoused was not without its weaknesses. Some of these weaknesses arise naturally out of his theological method, that of using reason apart from the revelation of God in Christ, as if Christ were not known. In setting forth the doctrine in this way, Anselm dissociated it from the love of God which is its source, a love which finds its concrete expression in the life and teaching of Jesus as well as in his death. The motive which Anselm stresses is not God's love for man, but that God's purpose in creation would be frustrated and God himself would be dishonored if God failed to redeem his handiwork. This view, if carried to its ultimate conclusion (which Anselm does not do), would lead to universalism, the view that every man eventually will be saved. Anselm's theological method also leads to a distorted view of the incarnation and a one-sided emphasis upon the death of Christ. Rightly understood, the incarnation is the presupposition of the atonement; but in Anselm's view atonement is the sole purpose of the incarnation. This leaves little room for the idea of the revelation of God in the incarnation. Anselm does make a passing reference to the uplifting effect of the example of Christ's death; but this is not an integral part of his argument, and it could hardly be argued that Anselm regards this as one of the purposes of the incarnation. Christ's life of obedience is taken for granted, and saving significance is attached solely to his death. The resurrection has no vital place in Anselm's view of the atonement, and the life of Christ is significant only as the necessary prelude to his death.[50]

Other weaknesses of Anselm's view of the atonement stem from the legalistic presuppositions upon which it is based. Anselm makes *"the principles of the practice of penance the fundamental scheme of religion in general."*[51] The term "satisfaction," which is the central term in Anselm's conception, was introduced into Christian theology by Tertullian, with reference to penance; and the whole background of the satisfaction view is the Roman Catholic practice of penance. The whole concept of the saving significance of the death of Christ as lying in its excess merit which God must reward rests squarely upon the legalism of Roman Catholic theological presuppositions. James Denny, who is, generally speaking, deeply sympathetic with Anselm's basic point of view, states the weakness in this way:

> Christ is left standing, so to speak, with the merit of His death in His hand, and looking around to see what He can do with it. What is more suitable or becoming (*covenientius*) than that He should give it to those who in virtue of the incarnation are His kindred?[52]

Anselm fails to make it clear that the appropriation of the atonement is conditioned by faith-union with Christ, by which in identification with Christ we are led to die to sin, and live

---

[50] Wolf, *op. cit.*, p. 107.

[51] Harnack, *op. cit.*, Vol. VI, p. 56. Italics in the original.

[52] James Denny, *The Christian Doctrine of Reconciliation* (London: James Clarke & Co., this edition, 1959), p. 77.

unto righteousness. The result is that though "Anselm's theory deals with God's judgment on sin. . . . It does not deal with the more radical problem of curing man of his sinfulness in a redeemed world."[53] In short, it lacks the dynamic for a new life.

Anselm's theory rests upon a view of God in which God, in his supreme concern for his own outraged honor, bears more resemblance to a feudal lord of the Middle Ages than to the God and Father of our Lord Jesus Christ. Aulén's basic criticism of Anselm and all Latin theories is that whereas in the "classic" view there is a continuity in the divine action, in the Latin view there is a discontinuity in divine action; and the atonement is offered to God by man as man.[54] Whether Aulén's criticism is valid or not is open to debate. But the type of thinking which Anselm sets forth easily leads to a conception of the atonement in which the Father and the Son are set over against each other. Carried to the extreme it evokes the reaction sometimes expressed, "I love Jesus, but I hate God!" Whereas the patristic view, in its extreme forms, tends to make the devil into a god, the Latin view, in its extreme forms, tends to turn God into a devil.[55]

III. ABELARD: THE MORAL INFLUENCE THEORY

Abelard's moral influence view of the atonement is best understood as a reaction against Anselm's satisfaction theory. Anselm had set forth the necessity of the atonement on the basis of sheer logic, apart from the historical revelation of God in Christ. In his explication of it he had made little reference to the love of God which prompted it and the love from man which it evokes. Abelard sought to correct this deficiency, but in doing so he rejected the primary theses upon which Anselm's view had been built.

Whereas Anselm's view had been based upon an interpretation of the Trinity which emphasizes strongly three persons in the Godhead and tends towards tritheism, Abelard's view was based upon an interpretation of the Trinity which denied personality distinctions within the Godhead and tended toward Sabellianism.[56] Anselm had taken for granted an Augustinian

---

53 Wolf, *op. cit.*, p. 108.
54 Aulén, *op. cit.*, pp. 83, 91.
55 Paul, *op. cit.*, p. 79.
56 Cf. Arthur Cushman McGiffert, *A History of Christian Thought* (New York: Charles Scribner's Sons, 1954), Vol. II, p. 212.

interpretation of original sin; but Abelard rejected this view, denying that mankind shares in the guilt of Adam's sin, and maintaining that if men have weaknesses which incline them to sin, they also have tendencies toward good.[57] Whereas Anselm had emphasized the purpose of the incarnation and the death of Christ as that of providing a satisfaction so as to make it possible for God to forgive sin without impairing the divine honor, "Abelard maintained that there was nothing in the nature of God to hinder the free exercise of forgiveness and that the only impediment to it was in men, not in God."[58]

Abelard (1079-1142 A.D.), the younger contemporary of Anselm, was a gifted theologian, whose love of debate often led him to challenge revered and well-established views, thus arousing the opposition of many of his contemporaries. Paradoxically enough, this man whose life was broken because of the tragic consequences of his love for Heloise, and whose theological career was lived out in the midst of controversy, became the greatest advocate of "that interpretation of the work of Christ which sees in it supremely love enkindling love."[59]

Abelard's treatment of the atonement is to be found chiefly in his *Epitome of Christian Theology* and his *Commentary on Romans.* Since the first book seems to have been compiled by Abelard's disciples after Abelard's death and probably contains views of the disciples as well as Abelard, the best source for the knowledge of Abelard's views on the subject is the second book.

Like Anselm, Abelard raised the question *Cur deus homo?* but his answer was quite different from Anselm's. Motivated by love toward us the Son of God assumed flesh that he might deliver us from the yoke of sin. In his life he illuminated us by his light and manifested his love toward us. "How great that love for us was, He showed in this that He laid down for us the life He had assumed."[60]

In his *Commentary on Romans* Abelard attacked both the patristic view of a ransom paid to the devil and Anselm's view of a satisfaction paid to God. He denied the premises on which the patristic view had been built, claiming that Satan had no right over man, and maintaining that God could have delivered

57 Kenneth Scott Latourette, *A History of Christianity* (New York: Harper and Row, 1953), p. 504.

58 McGiffert, *op. cit.,* p. 213.

59 Cave, *op. cit.,* p. 133.

60 *The Epitome of Christian Doctrine,* quoted by Cave, *op. cit.,* pp. 133-34.

man from the tortures of Satan simply by a command to Satan, without the Son of God going to the cross. Against the satisfaction view of the atonement Abelard raised such objections as the following. Did not men act more criminally in crucifying the Son of God than man did in Paradise through disobeying the command of God in the tasting of a single apple?

> And if that sin of Adam was so great that it could be expiated only by the blood of Christ, what expiation will avail for that act of murder committed against Christ. . . ?
> Indeed, how cruel and wicked it seems that anyone should demand the death of an innocent person as the price of anything, or that it should in any way please him that an innocent person should be slain — still less that God should consider the death of his Son so agreeable that by it he should be reconciled to the whole world![61]

Abelard was not the first to raise these objections. Anselm himself had anticipated them and attempted to answer them. He answered the objection concerning the sin of those who murdered Jesus by saying that it had been committed in ignorance and that Christ through his death had atoned even for the sin of these who murdered him.[62] The second of Abelard's objections had been voiced by Boso:

> For what justice is there in giving up the most just man of all to death on behalf of sinners? What man would not be judged worthy of condemnation if he condemned the innocent in order to free the guilty?[63]

To this Anselm countered by saying that Christ had voluntarily endured death in order to save men, an answer which only partially alleviates the difficulty.

Abelard's solution to the problem is indicated in quotations like the following:

> Now it seems to us that we have been justified by the blood of Christ and reconciled to God in this way: through this unique act of grace manifested to us — in that his Son has taken upon himself our nature and persevered therein in teaching us by word and example even unto death — he has the more fully bound us to himself by love; with the result that our

61 "Commentary on Romans," *LCC*, Vol. X, pp. 282-83.
62 *Cur Deus Homo?* II, 14, 15.
63 *Ibid.*, I, 8.

hearts should be enkindled by such a gift of divine grace, and
true charity should not now shrink from enduring anything
for him.

Wherefore, our redemption through Christ's suffering is that
deeper affection in us which not only frees us from slavery to
sin, but also wins for us the true liberty of sons of God, so
that we do all things out of love rather than fear. . . .[64]

In his treatment of the atonement Abelard repeatedly quotes
John 15:13. Moreover, he finds an illustration of the principle
of the atonement in Jesus' words concerning the sinful woman:
"Her sins, which are many, are forgiven, for she has loved
much" (Luke 7:47).

At times Abelard uses traditional language in interpreting
the atonement, speaking of the devil as demanding the precious
blood of Christ as the price of our liberation, or of Christ sup-
plementing our merits by his own, or even of his bearing our
punishment. However, such expressions are not the characteristic ones in his thought, and they are in reality inconsistent
with the main emphasis of his teaching. In short, Abelard's view
is that "Christ took on flesh and lived among men and died on
the cross in order to reveal the love of God and thus arouse
in them an answering love which is their reconciliation and
redemption."[65]

Abelard's views were attacked by Bernard of Clairvaux in a
letter to the pope; and without being given a chance to defend
himself, Abelard was condemned by the Council of Sins and
by the pope and excommunicated.

Abelard was correct in his positive affirmations that the incarnation and death of the Son of God are the supreme revelation of the love of God. This revelation becomes effective for
our salvation by evoking from us a response of faith and love.
In laying hold of this obvious scriptural truth Abelard corrected
what was perhaps the basic weakness of Anselm's view. The incarnation and the atonement obviously have this meaning,
but is this all? Rashdall, an ardent, twentieth-century advocate
of the Abelardian interpretation, correctly perceives that the
question at issue is not a matter of the truth of the Abelardian
view but of its sufficiency.[66]

[64] Abelard, "Commentary on Romans," *LCC,* Vol. X, pp. 283-84.
[65] McGiffert, *op. cit.,* Vol. II, p. 213.
[66] Rashdall, *op. cit.,* p. 438.

However, Abelard's view is weak in the very place where it is strong. As Denny aptly puts it, "The death of Christ can only be regarded as a demonstration of love to sinners, if it can be defined or interpreted as having some necessary relation to their sins."[67] It is in giving his Son to save us that God demonstrates his love. But in denying any objective element in the atonement and by ignoring the great body of scriptural teaching concerning Christ as the ransom for our sins and concerning his bearing our sins, the moral influence view inverts the order. According to Abelard, God saves us by revealing his love. But it is at this point that the moral influence view is most ambiguous. It fails to give an adequate explanation of how the death of Christ is a demonstration of God's love, because it fails to recognize the atonement as an objective act of God through which the sin of man is annulled. The subjective appropriation of the atonement depends upon the objective fact of the atonement.

Finally, the moral influence view "totally neglects the redemption of the past from the objective reality of guilt."[68] "It has little to say to the sinner who is oppressed with the sense of his own guilt for the sins of the past and conscious of his own inability to save himself from the sins of the present."[69]

IV. LUTHER: PENALTY AND VICTORY

Is the key to Luther's doctrine of the atonement penal substitution or the victory over the evil powers? Until Aulén wrote *Christus Victor* interpreters of Luther usually took it for granted that Luther's doctrine of the atonement is of the Latin type, and that there is a continuity of tradition running from Anselm through Luther to Lutheran orthodoxy. Aulén strongly contends, however, that "Luther's teaching can only be rightly understood as a revival of the old classic theme of the Atonement as taught by the Fathers, but with a greater depth of treatment."[70] In this position Aulén has the strong backing of an influential school of Swedish Luther scholars.[71]

---

[67] Denny, *The Christian Doctrine of Reconciliation*, p. 78.

[68] Wolf, *op. cit.*, p. 150.

[69] Paul, *op. cit.*, p. 83.

[70] Aulén, *op. cit.*, p. 102.

[71] Cf. Edgar M. Carlson, *The Reinterpretation of Luther* (Philadelphia: The Westminster Press, 1948), especially Chapter III.

Aulén bases his argument not only upon the fact that vivid imagery of a dramatic struggle with the evil powers and victory over them occurs frequently in Luther's hymns, theological writings, and particularly in his catechisms, where he is aiming at precision of statement, but also on the contention that Luther's doctrine of the atonement is an integral part of his whole structure of thought, and that the Christus Victor theme gives to his theology an inner harmony, while the Latin doctrine of the atonement would introduce an antinomy into his thought. Aulén says:

> The presupposition of the Latin theory was the moralistic idea of penance; but that was for Luther an abomination. The Latin doctrine involved the idea of law and justice as the typical expression of God's relation to man; but this is just what Luther tears in pieces, raising God's claim to a higher level, and therefore treating Law as, in one aspect, a tyrant from which man needs to be delivered. The structure of the Latin theory is rational throughout; Luther, if he is sure of anything, is sure that God's work in Christ of atonement, forgiveness, justification, bears the signature *contra rationem et legem*.[72]

Here again, Christian theology is indebted to Aulén. The Christus Victor theme is certainly an important one in Luther's treatment of the atonement; and, until Aulén emphasized it, it had seldom been given due stress in interpretations of Luther.

Martin Luther (1483-1546 A.D.) thought in dualistic terms. To him the devil was real, as his hymns clearly indicate. The devil has led man into disobedience, because of which man is under the wrath of God and doomed to eternal damnation.

> There was no counsel, help or comfort until this only-begotten and eternal Son of God in his unfathomable goodness had compassion upon our misery and wretchedness, and came from heaven to help us. Thus therefore the tyrants and jailers are all expelled, and in their stead stands Jesus Christ, Lord of Life, righteousness, salvation and of all good, and who delivered us poor lost mortals from the jaws of hell, has redeemed us and made us free, and brought us again into the favor and grace of the Father. . . .[73]

[72] *Op. cit.*, pp. 120-21.
[73] "The Large Catechism," II, 2, *The Book of Concord*, Henry E. Jacobs, editor (Philadelphia: The United Lutheran Publication House, 1908), Vol. I, p. 442.

In depicting Christ's victory over the devil Luther does not hesitate to use the most grotesque imagery of the fathers. The devil, like a greedy fish, tries to devour the bait of the humanity of Christ; but in doing so he is caught on the hook of Christ's deity, which is concealed by his humanity. This is the divine wisdom whereby the power of the devil is overthrown.[74]

To the evil powers of sin, death, and the devil, about which the fathers frequently speak, Luther adds the law, and even the wrath of God. Over all of these personified evils Christ has won the decisive victory. "Therefore if thou look upon this person (Christ), thou shalt see sin, death, the wrath of God, hell, the devil and all evils vanquished and mortified (in him)."[75]

Luther emphasizes the deity of Christ, making it clear that the victory is from God, not from man. No creature, but only one who was truly and naturally God, could overcome sin, death and the curse. Thus against these mighty forces it was necessary for God to set a mightier power — his own.[76]

But the Christus Victor theme is not the only one in Luther. At least as prominent as this theme, and probably more so, is the idea of Christ as our penal substitute, who bears our sins, becomes sin for us, accepts the punishment which we justly deserve, and delivers us from sin, death, the devil, the curse of the law, and the wrath of God. Aulén, in his eagerness to correct what he regards as a distorted interpretation of Luther, does not do justice to this aspect of Luther's teaching, and thus introduces a distortion of a different kind. Aulén fails to make a clear distinction between the satisfaction theory of Anselm and the view of penal substitution espoused by Luther and Calvin and their followers. It is true, as Aulén rightly perceives, that Luther does not think in Anselm's terms of Christ as man making an offering to God, or of some special merit as residing solely in his death and transferable to man's account. But he does think of Christ as becoming sin for us, as enduring the curse which the law rightly pronounces on sin, and thus as de-

---

[74] *The Table-Talk of Martin Luther,* translated by William Hazlitt (Philadelphia: The Lutheran Publication Society), CXCVII, pp. 105-06.

[75] Martin Luther, *A Commentary on St. Paul's Epistle to the Galatians,* based on lectures delivered by Luther at the University of Wittenberg in 1531 and first published in 1535 (London: James Clarke & Co., second impression, 1956), p. 274.

[76] *Loc. cit.*

livering us from it. It is this important aspect of Luther's teaching which Aulén neglects.

The heart of Luther's theology of the cross is found in Isaiah 53:6; Galatians 3:13; and II Corinthians 5:21. Luther quotes these passages continually and interprets them in the most literalistic fashion. Luther speaks of Christ as accursed and as the greatest of sinners.

> He verily is innocent, because he is the unspotted and undefiled Lamb of God. But because he beareth the sins of the world, his innocence is burdened with the sins and guilt of the whole world. Whatsoever sins, I, thou, and we all have done, or shall do hereafter, they are Christ's own sins as verily as if he himself had done them. To be brief: our sins must needs become Christ's own sin, or else we shall perish for ever.[77]

Luther represents Christ as saying, "I have committed the sins which all men have committed."[78]

> To conclude, all evils should have overwhelmed us, as they shall overwhelm the wicked for ever: but Christ being made for us a transgressor of all laws, guilty of all our maledictions, our sins, and all our evils, cometh between as a mediator.[79]
>
> For God hath laid our sins, not upon us, but upon his Son Christ that he bearing the punishment thereof might be our peace, and that by his stripes we might be healed (Isa. liii. 5).[80]

Luther speaks of an exchange in which Christ accepts our sin and death, and we receive his righteousness and life. "So making a happy change with us, he took upon him our sinful person, and gave unto us his innocent and victorious person. . . ."[81] This exchange does not take place mechanically, but is effected by faith, which unites the soul to Christ, as a bride is united with her bridegroom. Thereby the sin, death, and condemnation which belong to the bride become the bridegroom's, and the grace, life, and salvation which belong to the bridegroom become the bride's.[82]

In the elaboration of the theme of Christ as our penal sub-

---

[77] *Ibid.*, p. 270.
[78] *Ibid.*, p. 275.
[79] *Ibid.*, p. 281.
[80] *Ibid.*, p. 271.
[81] *Ibid.*, p. 276.
[82] *Works of Luther*, six-volume edition (Philadelphia: Muhlenberg Press, 1943), Vol. II, pp. 320-21.

stitute, Luther speaks of Christ as enduring the full intensity of the wrath of God[83] and of his becoming the ransom for our sins, through which God is reconciled to us.[84] Nevertheless, he recognizes the sacrifice of Christ as God's gift to man, as having originated in the love of God, and as God's supreme demonstration of his love to man.[85]

Which theme is dominant in Luther, penal substitution or victory over the evil powers? Luther makes no attempt to give a concise, consistent theological system elaborating the doctrine of the atonement. The nearest approach to this is found in his *Commentary on Galatians* in his interpretation of Galatians 3: 13. Here he vigorously sets forth both ideas. At times Luther seems to indicate that Christ is the victor over sin, death, the devil, the law, and the wrath of God because he bore the curse of all of these in his own body. Satan no longer has power to terrify the believer when the believer remembers that all of his sins have been laid upon Christ the Redeemer.[86] At times, however, he seems to indicate that the victory is due to the fact that Christ in his deity overcame death and all the evil powers through the resurrection.[87] In one passage Luther links together the incarnation, the death, and the resurrection of Jesus and interprets these dramatic events in terms both of penal substitution and victory over the evil powers.

> So in one person he joineth God and man together, and being united unto us which were accursed, he was made a curse for us, and hid his blessings in our sin, in our death, and in our curse, which condemned him and put him to death. But because he was the Son of God, he could not be holden of them, but overcame them, (led them captive) and triumphed over them; and whatsoever did hang upon the flesh, which for our sake he took upon him, he carried it with him. Wherefore all they that cleave unto this flesh, are blessed and delivered from the curse, that is, from sin and everlasting death.[88]

---

[83] *Table-Talk*, CXCVI, p. 104.

[84] "Epistle Sermon, Twenty-fourth Sunday after Trinity," *The J. N. Lenker Edition of Luther's Works* (Minneapolis: The Luther Press), Vol. IX, No. 43-45.

[85] *Table-Talk*, XCIII, pp. 120-21; *Commentary on Galatians*, p. 283.

[86] *Commentary on Galatians*, p. 51; cf. pp. 276, 279.

[87] *Ibid.*, pp. 273, 281.

[88] *Ibid.*, p. 281.

Luther's is the truest and most profound interpretation of the atonement that we have dealt with thus far. Anselm had attached atoning significance to the death of Christ alone, giving no significance to the resurrection. Moreover, he had failed to make it clear that it is only by being united to Christ by faith that we can appropriate this salvation. The note of victory that rings throughout Luther's treatment of the subject is hardly sounded in Anselm. All of these weaknesses are overcome in Luther's interpretation.

However, Luther is too literalistic in his interpretations and too extreme in his expressions. This applies both to the grotesque imagery which he uses in portraying Christ's victory over the devil and to his representation of Christ as the greatest of sinners. Whether sin and guilt can be transferred in the manner that Luther describes is doubtful. Though Luther emphasizes the love of God in delivering up his Son for us all, in Luther's representation of the atonement, Aulén's interpretation notwithstanding, there seems to be a cleavage between the Father and the Son, with the Father inflicting punishment and the Son enduring it.

V. Calvin and Calvinism: Sacrifice and Penal Substitute

Luther never attempted a single, consistent, systematic interpretation of the Christian faith. But this deficiency of the great German reformer, if it may be regarded as such, was made up for by John Calvin (1509-1564 A.D.), the younger contemporary of Luther. Calvin's doctrine of the atonement is set forth with remarkable clarity, consistency, and simplicity in Book II of his *Institutes of the Christian Religion.* Calvin's commentaries amplify the subject at various points, but they add nothing essential to Calvin's view as found in the *Institutes.*

The necessity of redemption arises from the fact of sin and corruption in which the whole human race has been involved by the sin of Adam. Since man in his sin has cut himself off from God, the only way back to God is the way which God himself has provided in sending his Son as the Mediator. The purpose of the incarnation was that of propitiating God and of providing a way of salvation for lost man, and it is both absurd and unscriptural to say that the incarnation would have taken place even if man had not sinned. The work to be performed by the Mediator was "to restore us to divine favour, so as to make us, instead of sons of men, sons of God; instead of heirs of hell, heirs of a heavenly kingdom."[89]

It was necessary for the Mediator to be both truly God and truly man. Since his work was that of swallowing up death and conquering sin, the Redeemer must be life and righteousness; in other words, God Himself. "Therefore God, in his infinite mercy, having determined to redeem us, became himself our Redeemer in the person of his only-begotten Son.[90]" Since man in the person of Adam had disobeyed God and fallen into sin, our Lord in order to overcome the effects of this disobedience

> came forth very man, adopted the person of Adam, and assumed his name, that he might in his stead obey the Father; that he might present our flesh as the price of satisfaction to the just judgment of God, and in the same flesh pay the penalty which we had incurred.[91]

God cannot suffer and die, and man cannot conquer death; but by combining divinity and humanity in one person, the Mediator endured death as the expiation of sin, and gained for us the victory over death through his conquest of it.[92]

The Mediator is called Christ, "the Anointed," because he has been anointed by God to the offices of prophet, king, and priest. The prophetic office refers to his preaching and teaching ministry, to his revelation of God. The kingly office refers to his reign, which Calvin interprets in a spiritual sense. The priestly office refers to his atonement for sin. In the exercise of this office, Christ is both the priest and the sacrifice. He is the sacrifice, because no other fit satisfaction for sin could be found. And he is the priest, for no one else was worthy of the honor of offering an only-begotten Son to God.[93]

It is in the context of the priestly ministry of Christ that Calvin arrives at the heart of his explication of the atonement, and he sets it forth in terms of the framework of the Apostles' Creed.[94] All of us, both because of our corrupt nature and our depraved conduct, have that in us which deserves the hatred of

---

[89] *Institutes of the Christian Religion,* translated by Henry Beveridge (Grand Rapids: Wm. B. Eerdmans Publishing Co., 1957), II, xii, 2.

[90] *Ibid.,* II, xii, 2.

[91] *Ibid.,* II, xii, 3.

[92] *Ibid.,* II, xii, 3.

[93] *Ibid.,* II, xv, 6.

[94] *Ibid.,* II, xvi.

God. Since God is perfect righteousness, he cannot love the iniquity which he sees in us. But despite the fact that we are sinners, because we are still his creatures, mere gratuitous love prompts God to receive us into favor. But God can do this only by removing in us the ground of offence; that is, by the expiation that is set forth in the death of Christ abolishing all the evil that is in us, "so that we, formerly impure and unclean, now appear in his sight just and holy."[95] Calvin quotes with approval such passages of Scripture as Romans 5:8, 10 and John 3:16 to show that the love of God is the ground of the atonement, that it "is because he first loves us, that he afterwards reconciles us to himself."[96] Calvin lets Augustine speak for him:

> 'For it was not after we were reconciled to him by the blood of his Son that he began to love us, but he loved us before the foundation of the world, that with his only begotten Son we too might be sons of God before we were anything at all. . . . Accordingly, in a manner wondrous and divine, he loved us even when he hated us. For he hated us when we were such as he had not made us, and yet because our iniquity had not destroyed his work in every respect, he knew in regard to each one of us, both to hate what we had made, and love what he had made.'[97]

Calvin emphasizes the obedience of Christ as that which abolishes sin and purchases righteousness. "As by one man's disobedience many were made sinners, so by the obedience of one shall many be made righteous" (Rom. 5:15). The obedience of Christ, which secures our righteousness, extended throughout his life. In this sense it is proper to say that from the time he took the form of a servant he began to pay the price of our redemption. However, the Scriptures assign saving significance particularly to the death of Christ (Matt. 20:28; Rom. 3:25; 5:9; Phil. 2:7).

Calvin interprets the death of Christ both in terms of the forensic category of penal substitution and the sacrificial category of a sacrifice for sins which renders God propitious toward us. That Jesus was condemned before Pontius Pilate and made to die the death of a criminal on a cross has for Calvin a special significance. "He was numbered with the transgressors"

95 *Ibid.*, II, xvi, 3.
96 *Ibid.*, II, xvi, 3, 4.
97 *Ibid.*, II, xvi, 4. (Cf. Augustine, Tract in John 110.)

(Isa. 53:12; Mark 15:28), and died the death of a criminal that it might be manifest that he met death not on account of innocence, but of sin. But Pilate who condemned him, nevertheless bore public testimony to his innocence.

> Thus we perceive Christ representing the character of a sinner and a criminal, while, at the same time, his innocence shines forth, and it becomes manifest that he suffers for another's and not for his own crime.[98]

"Our acquittal is in this — that the guilt which made us liable to punishment was transferred to the head of the Son of God (Isa. liii. 12)."[99] Calvin quotes such passages as Isaiah 53:5, 10; II Corinthians 5:21; Romans 8:3; Galatians 3:13, 14; and I Peter 2:24 to show that "Christ, in his death, was offered to the Father as a propitiatory victim."[100] According to Calvin, the guilt and penalty of our sin is laid on Christ, the propitiatory victim, and thus it ceases to be imputed to us. In this manner Calvin combines the forensic and sacrificial categories. "For the Son of God, though spotlessly pure, took upon him the disgrace and ignominy of our iniquities, and in return clothed us with his purity."[101]

The Apostles' Creed mentions that Christ was "dead and buried." "Death held us under its yoke, but he in our place delivered himself into its power, that he might exempt us from it."[102] He tasted death for every man (Heb. 2:9). Moreover, he triumphed over him who has the power of death and freed us from his bondage (Heb. 2:14-15). "An effect of his burial, moreover, is, that we as his fellows are buried to sin."[103]

To Calvin the reference to the descent into hell in the Apostles' Creed has a profound meaning. According to his interpretation, it does not have reference to what happened to Christ after he died and was buried. The references in the Apostles' Creed to Christ's suffering under Pontius Pilate, to his dying and being buried, indicate what he endured in the sight of men. However, the reference to the descent into hell in the Creed refers to the "incomprehensible judgment which

---

[98] *Ibid.*, II, xvi, 5.
[99] *Ibid.*, II, xvi, 5.
[100] *Ibid.*, II, xvi, 6.
[101] *Ibid.*, II, xvi, 6.
[102] *Ibid.*, II, xvi, 7.
[103] *Ibid.*, II, xvi, 7.

he endured before God."[104] Calvin interprets this descent into hell to mean that "he endured the death which is inflicted on the wicked by an angry God," that "he bore in his soul the tortures of condemned and ruined man."[105] The corporeal death of God's Son would never have been sufficient to satisfy God's righteous judgment. This could be accomplished only as the Son endured the weight of divine vengeance, engaging "at close quarters with the power of hell and the horrors of eternal death."[106]

In the next two sections Calvin gives a profound interpretation to the agonies of Jesus in Gethsemane and the cry of dereliction from the cross: "My God, my God, why hast thou forsaken me?"

> It is evident that the expression was wrung from the anguish of his inmost soul. We do not, however, insinuate that God was ever hostile to him or angry with him. How could he be angry with the beloved Son, with whom his soul was well pleased? Or how could he have appeased the Father by his intercession for others if He were hostile to himself? But this we say, that he bore the weight of the divine anger, that smitten and afflicted, he experienced all the signs of an angry and avenging God.[107]

It is only through such an interpretation that we can understand the agonies of Jesus in Gethsemane and his cry of dereliction from the cross. And it is only through a correct interpretation of these that we see how much our salvation cost the Son of God. "Had not his soul shared in the punishment, he would have been a Redeemer of bodies only."[108]

> Thus by engaging with the power of the devil, the fear of death, and the pains of hell, he gained the victory, and achieved a triumph, so that we now fear not in death those things which our Prince has destroyed.[109]

Calvin brings the victory of the cross into closest proximity with the resurrection, as is done in the Apostles' Creed, for it is through the resurrection that this victory is revealed. By the death of Christ sin was abolished and death annihilated, while

104 *Ibid.*, II, xvi, 10.
105 *Ibid.*, II, xvi, 10.
106 *Ibid.*, II, xvi, 10.
107 *Ibid.*, II, xvi, 11.
108 *Ibid.*, II, xvi, 12.
109 *Ibid.*, II, xvi, 11.

by the resurrection righteousness was restored and life revived, the power and efficacy of the cross being dependent upon the resurrection.[110]

Calvin then treats the ascension, the reign of Christ at God's right hand, the second coming and the judgment — all of which are mentioned in the Apostles' Creed; and he concludes that since the sum of our salvation and every single part of it are from Christ, we must beware of seeking it in any other quarter.[111]

In chapter xvii Calvin stresses the idea that Christ by his sacrifice has merited grace and salvation for us. Again and again he emphasizes the love of God as the source of the gift of the Son, underscoring such passages as John 3:16; Romans 5:8; 8:32; I John 4:10. He quotes I John 4:10, stressing the word "propitiation." "There is great force in this word *propitiation;* for in a manner which cannot be expressed, God, at the very time when he loved us, was hostile to us until reconciled in Christ."[112]

Although Christ suffered for the salvation of the human race, his death has no saving efficacy for us until the Holy Spirit awakens faith in us and by it unites us to Christ.[113] Calvin defines faith as "the knowledge of the divine will in regard to us, as ascertained from his word."[114] This faith is the gift of God, and the hope of eternal life is its inseparable companion.[115] True faith issues in repentance,[116] but this faith has its ultimate ground in the divine election.[117]

A comparison and contrast of the views of Calvin and Anselm should be instructive. Both emphasize the atonement as the purpose of the incarnation. Moreover, both ground the necessity of the atonement in the nature of God himself. While in Anselm the emphasis is upon the honor of God, in Calvin it is upon the justice of God. Whereas Anselm poses the alternative satisfaction or punishment, for Calvin the issue is one of satisfaction through punishment. Whereas Anselm seeks to set forth the necessity of the atonement on the basis of pure logic apart from the revelation of God in Christ, Calvin seeks to make

110 *Ibid.,* II, xvi, 13.
111 *Ibid.,* II, xvi, 14-19.
112 *Ibid.,* II, xvii, 2.
113 *Ibid.,* III, i, 1-4.
114 *Ibid.,* III, ii, 6.
115 *Ibid.,* II, ii, 33, 42.
116 *Ibid.,* III, iii.
117 *Ibid.,* III, xxi-xxiv.

clear the nature of the atonement on the basis of the revelation of God in Christ. The result is that Calvin is more biblical than Anselm, not only in regard to method, but in regard to content as well. Calvin, unlike Anselm, treats the atonement as rooted in the love of God and flowing from it. Calvin, unlike Anselm, does not view the atonement as centered solely in the death of Christ, but sees Christ's life of obedience and his resurrection, as well as his death, as having saving significance. Finally, Calvin, unlike Anselm, deals with the method of the appropriation of the benefits of the atonement, regarding these as conditioned by a faith which unites us to Christ, a faith which is the gift of the Holy Spirit.

The similarities between Calvin's and Luther's interpretations of the atonement are striking, for both emphasize penal substitution. However, Calvin's statements are more moderate in tone and more systematic in treatment than Luther's. Calvin takes much more care to safeguard the moral purity of Christ in his interpretation than does Luther. Calvin's main emphasis is upon Christ as enduring the penalty of our sins, whereas in Luther's treatment the emphasis upon Christ as enduring the penalty of our sins is based upon the presupposition, accented again and again, that Christ literally became sin for us. Luther has a much greater stress upon the victory of Christ than does Calvin, though this aspect of the atonement is not neglected by Calvin. Calvin places a much greater emphasis upon the sacrificial aspect of the atonement than does Luther, interpreting the death of Christ as a propitiation, and setting forth the atoning work of Christ within the framework of Christ's discharge of his high priestly function.

Calvin's doctrine of the atonement is truly a milestone in Christian theology. Though Eusebius had spoken of the three-fold office of Christ, it was Calvin who elaborated it and made it the framework for the comprehensive interpretation of the work of Christ. Perhaps the greatest error in Calvin's view is the way the reformer interprets sacrifice in terms of propitiation instead of expiation, and assumes that the essence of sacrifice is the punishment of sin in a substitute. If the interpretation which we gave to sacrifice in the discussion of the Old Testament background of the atonement in the first chapter of this book is correct, then Calvin's interpretation is a gross misrepresentation of the meaning and purpose of sacrifice. Not vicarious punishment, but the dedication of life is the rationale by which sacrifice is to be interpreted.

Many of the criticisms commonly leveled at the view of penal substitution are really not so much criticisms of Calvin's view as distortions of his view in later Calvinism. Calvin specifically says that God does not love us because Christ died for us, but that Christ died for us because God loves us, and that God was not angry with the Son in whom he was well pleased. However, despite Calvin's attempts to erect safeguards against such errors, there are tendencies in this direction inherent within his theological position; and Calvin's disciples were not slow in ignoring Calvin's safeguards and in following the tendencies inherent in Calvin's position to their ultimate conclusion.

In later Calvinism there is a tendency to emphasize the retributive justice of God, making the punishment of sin the primary requirement of God's nature. Love and mercy, in comparison, are optional qualities, but retributive justice is that without which God would not be God. There is a tendency to represent Jesus as the loving Son who comes in between us and the wrath of an angry God, thus enabling God to forgive us and shower his love upon us. In so interposing himself between us and God's anger, Jesus himself becomes the object of the wrath of God. Many reformed theologians follow through the logic of Calvin's double predestination and interpret the atonement as limited in its purpose, meaning that Christ died only for the elect. This position is also arrived at on the basis of a supposed exact equivalence between the punishment endured by Christ and the sin for which he atoned. Against all such distortions of biblical teaching Christian theology must take its stand.

VI. Socinus: The Example View

The founder of the Socinian movement was Faustus Socinus (1539-1604 A.D.); but he owed much to his uncle, Lelius Socinus, who died leaving manuscripts which he had not dared to publish. Faustus Socinus did not publish these manuscripts, but he drew inspiration from them for his own attacks on the doctrine of the Trinity and the satisfaction theory of the atonement. The best sources for an understanding of the Socinian doctrine of the atonement are Faustus Socinus' *De Jesu Christo Servatore*, published in 1594, and the *Racovian Catechism*, the

work of Faustus and his friends and disciples, which was pub-
blished in 1605, a year after Socinus' death.

In the opening chapter of *De Jesu Christo Servatore* Socinus
sets forth his basic point of view:

> The common and, as you would say, orthodox view is, that
> Jesus Christ is our Saviour, because He made full satisfaction for
> our sins to the divine justice through which we sinners deserved
> to be condemned, and this satisfaction is through faith imputed
> by the gift of God to us who believe. But I hold, and think it
> to be the orthodox view, that Jesus Christ is our Saviour be-
> cause he announced to us the way of eternal salvation, confirmed,
> and in His own person, both by the example of His life and
> by rising from the dead, clearly showed it (i.e. eternal life) , and
> will give that eternal life to us who have faith in Him. And
> I affirm that He did not make satisfaction for our sins to the
> divine justice . . . nor was there any need that He should make
> satisfaction.[118]

The powerful arguments which Faustus Socinus directed
against the satisfaction view of the atonement have been used
again and again by the opponents of such interpretations of the
atonement as were set forth by Anselm and Calvin. Some of
Socinus' chief arguments, succinctly stated, are as follows. There
is nothing in the nature of God which requires the punishment
of sin. Neither justice nor mercy is absolute, but the will of
God; and God is free to forgive or punish sin as he wills. If
God punishes sin or requires satisfaction, he does not forgive,
for these are two mutually exclusive alternatives. It is unjust
to punish the innocent and let the guilty go free. If it were
necessary for God to punish someone, he should have punished
the guilty, not the innocent. Since eternal death is the penalty
of sin, the death of Christ cannot be efficacious in removing
this penalty, since Jesus did not suffer eternal death. Moreover,
even if Jesus had suffered eternal death, his death as the penalty
for sin would have been efficacious for only one person, since
he could suffer only one eternal death. Since Christ did not
suffer in his divine nature, his sufferings do not have infinite
worth. It is absurd to think that the sins of the sinner can be
transferred to Christ, or the righteousness of Christ be transferred to the sinner. Christ owed complete obedience to God
for himself, and so his obedience cannot be transferred to us.

[118] Quoted by Cave, *op. cit.*, pp. 172-73.

The New Testament teachings which seem to interpret the death of Christ in terms of satisfaction for sin are to be interpreted metaphorically. Christ bore our sins in the sense "that he took them away from us by inciting us to abandon them."[119]

Briefly stated, Socinus' view is that Christ "becomes our saviour by making known the way of eternal salvation and that we may reach that goal by imitating him."[120] Others in following Christ may have to suffer martyrdom. This Jesus suffered first. Christ's power to save is based upon the truth of his teaching and the influence of his example. Moreover, his teachings are confirmed by his resurrection from the dead.

If Socinus had been as proficient in stating a constructive view of the atonement as he was in assailing the prevailing view, his contribution to Christian theology would have been tremendous indeed. Unfortunately, however, the untenability of his general theological position made it impossible for him to make such a constructive contribution. There is, of course, truth in the view that Christ in his obedience even unto death is an example for others to follow (I Pet. 2:21-23; Matt. 16:24). However, this is far from being an adequate explanation of the atonement.

Socinus' view of the saving work of Christ is connected with a mistaken Christology and a strong anti-Trinitarian view of God. In Socinus' view, though Christ was born of a virgin, lived a holy life, performed miracles, and rose from the dead, he is not the unique incarnation of God, for the divinity of Christ is denied.

Though Socinus speaks of Christ as Saviour, it is doubtful if, on the basis of his premises, Christ should be so regarded. Salvation is ultimately by self-effort in following the example of Christ, not by the power of another. This is all based on a Pelagian interpretation of man and sin, which underestimates the seriousness of sin and overestimates the power of the human will to carry out its purposes.

VII. Grotius: The Governmental View

The Socinian attack on Calvinistic orthodoxy soon provoked a counterattack. Strangely enough, this came from the Armin-

---

[119] George Barker Stevens, *The Christian Doctrine of Salvation* (New York: Charles Scribner's Sons, 1905), p. 159.

[120] Latourette, *op. cit.*, p. 793.

ian camp in the form of a book called *Defense of the Catholic Faith on the Satisfaction of Christ against Faustus Socinus,* written by the learned Dutch jurist of international reputation, Hugo Grotius (1583-1645 A.D.). Grotius begins his book with what he regards as a definition of Catholic (universal) doctrine:

> God was moved by his own goodness to bestow distinguished blessings upon us. But since our sins, which deserved punishment, were an obstacle to this, he determined that Christ, being willing of his own love toward men, should, by bearing the most severe tortures, and a bloody and ignominious death, pay the penalty for our sins, in order that without prejudice to the exhibition of the divine justice, we might be liberated, upon the intervention of a true faith, from the punishment of eternal death.[121]

Grotius used much of the terminology of the view of penal substitution, speaking of Christ as appeasing the wrath of God, of his reconciling God to us, of his bearing our sins, of his satisfying divine justice, etc. Nevertheless, despite Grotius' avowed intention to defend the prevailing view from the Socinian attack, in reality he set forth a new view, which steers something of a middle course between the Calvinistic view on the one hand and the Socinian view on the other.

Grotius' basic presupposition is that God is to be regarded as a moral governor who always acts in the best interests of his subjects. A good governor cannot allow his subjects to sin with impunity, for to do so would be to encourage them to continue in sin. Even so, God in the forgiveness of our sins must mediate his forgiveness in such a way as to indicate the seriousness of sin and his displeasure at sin. Thus Jesus died as a penal example, an exhibition of God's displeasure concerning our sins, in order to deter us from sin. The law of Genesis 2:17 is that death should follow sin. If this law were rigorously applied, however, "two most beauteous things would utterly have perished — on the part of men religion towards God, on the part of God the proof of his special benevolence toward men."[122] These two weighty considerations caused God to relax his law. But as a proof of God's hatred of sin, and "that the law's authority might not be endangered by the entire abrogation of punish-

---

121 F. H. Foster's translation, 1880. Quoted by Stevens, *op. cit.,* p. 162.
122 The words of Grotius. Quoted by Mozley, *op. cit.,* p. 153.

ment,"[123] God punished man's sin in Christ. It was not unjust in this case for the innocent to be punished for the guilty because Christ voluntarily accepted the punishment, and he had the power in himself to accept it.

Grotius' view differs from the Calvinistic view in several important ways. In Grotius' interpretation, love, not justice, is the dominant quality of God. There is no quality of retributive justice in God which demands satisfaction for sin by punishment or an equivalent of punishment. The idea of an equivalence of sin and punishment drops out of consideration, as do the concepts of the imputation of the sinner's sins to Christ and of Christ's righteousness to the sinner. In contrast with the Calvinistic view, "The concern of this theory is not the expiation of divine justice, but its manifestation; its interest is prospective, not retrospective."[124]

As a mediating view between the penal substitution view of Calvin and his followers and the moral influence and example views of Abelard and Socinus, Grotius' view has exercised great influence upon theological thought. It exercised a pronounced influence upon Arminian theologians, particularly in England, and was set forth in one form or another by Daniel Whitby (1638-1726), Samuel Clarke (1675-1728), and Richard Watson (1781-1833). In America it was accepted in part by Jonathan Edwards, Sr., and almost in whole by Jonathan Edwards, Jr.; and through such Calvinists as these "the Grotian principles and method of thought became so general as to be regarded as characteristic of New England theology."[125] The influence of Grotius is clearly discernible also in the interpretation of the atonement given by such distinguished Scottish theologians as J. McLeod Campbell in the nineteenth century and H. R. Mackintosh in the twentieth.

The great strength of Grotius' view is that it makes it clear that "God who is holy love so forgives as in forgiveness to make sin abhorrent to us."[126] The basic weaknesses of the view are that it uses traditional terminology with nontraditional meaning, that it fails to make it clear how through the death of Christ the sinner's past is freed from the objective power of guilt, and that it is easily susceptible to the criticism that in the

123 Mozley, *op. cit.*, p. 153.
124 Cave, *op. cit.*, p. 177.
125 Stevens, *op. cit.*, p. 172.
126 Cave, *op. cit.*, p. 181.

atonement God works on the basis of what is expedient rather
than what is just. This has sometimes led theologians to cari-
cature Grotius' view by describing it in terms of Caiaphas' statement that it is expedient that one man should die for the people
and that the whole nation should not perish (John 11:50).

VIII. THE MODERN PERIOD: THE NINETEENTH AND TWENTIETH CENTURIES

The treatments of the atonement in the modern period are so
numerous that it would be entirely impractical to deal with
each theologian separately. Fortunately, this is not necessary,
however, for the theologians of this period, for the most part,
instead of setting forth completely new views, simply adopt or
adapt one or more of the views which we have already discussed.
Perhaps the best way to deal with the subject is that of classi-
fying some of the leading theologians according to the type
view they represent. It must be remembered, however, that this
is not an entirely satisfactory method, because some theologians
in their treatment of the subject combine different categories
of thought in such a way as to make it difficult to classify their
views. Again the matter of the selection of the theologians to
be included poses a problem, but for this choice as well as for
the discussion of the views treated, the writer must assume
full responsibility. Five different types of views will be dealt
with: views of satisfaction or penal substitution, views of moral
influence, views of vicarious confession or vicarious penitence,
views of sacrifice, and views of victory over the evil powers.

1. Views of Satisfaction or Penal Substitution

Some theologians of this period have not hesitated to set
forth the atonement in terms of the most rigid forms of seven-
teenth-century Calvinism. Among these should be included
Charles Hodge,[127] W. G. T. Shedd,[128] and L. Berkhof,[129] and, to
a lesser degree, T. J. Crawford[130] and A. H. Strong.[131] All of
these theologians regard the essential element in the atonement
as the vicarious punishment of sin in Christ, our substitute.

---

127 *Systematic Theology*, 3 vols., 1871.
128 *Dogmatic Theology*, 2 vols., 1889.
129 *Systematic Theology*, 1941.
130 *The Doctrine of Holy Scripture Respecting the Atonement*, second
edition, 1874.
131 *Systematic Theology*, 1907 edition.

All of them, moreover, argue that retributive justice, or holiness which demands the punishment of sin, is the most important element in the character of God, and that, if the Lawgiver so ordains, he can punish his innocent Son in the place of guilty man. All of them maintain that the atonement was intended to propitiate God and reconcile him to the sinner. Generally speaking, the theological positions of these men assume that there is some division within the divine nature, with the love of God being in conflict with the righteousness of God until the two are harmonized in the death of Christ. According to Shedd, "God's own mercy satisfies his own justice for the transgressor."[132] Some degree of separation between the Father and the Son is implicit within the view under discussion; but this is more evident in the first three theologians named than in Crawford and Strong, who through their cautious language attempt to preserve the concept of the unity of the Father and the Son. The imputation of the sinner's sins to Christ and of Christ's righteousness to the ·sinner is an integral part of the thought of these five theologians. Hodge and Berkhof apply the Calvinistic idea of predestination to the problem under discussion and arrive at the idea of limited atonement, that Christ died for the elect only. Crawford, Shedd, and Strong, however, maintain that Christ died for all, but that not all appropriate the benefits of his death.

Generally speaking, the theological position enunciated above is offensive to the moral sensibilities of modern man, and relatively few theologians today hold this position in its unmitigated form.

An attempt to restate the doctrine of penal substitution in such a way as not to offend the moral sensibilities of modern man was made by the great English preacher-theologian, R. W. Dale.[133] The reverent tone, charitable spirit, and profound scholarship displayed in this volume have made it a book which theologians, regardless of whether they accept or reject Dale's position, have been unable to ignore.

Refusing to use the proof-text method, but treating the teachings of the New Testament with deep understanding, Dale seeks to establish the fact that, according to the New

132 *Op. cit.*, Vol. II, p. 445.
133 R. W. Dale, *The Atonement* (London: Congregational Union of England and Wales, first edition, 1875, seventh edition, 1878, twenty-sixth edition, 1914) .

Testament, the remission of sins rests upon the objective fact
of Christ's death. Recognizing that faith in the fact of the atonement is far more important than the acceptance of any theory,[134]
and that the New Testament itself does not give us the theory of
the atonement but simply illustrations of the atonement which
may be used in testing the validity of a theory,[135] he nevertheless
proceeds to construct a theory along the lines of penal substitution. Dale repudiates the idea that punishment is corrective
in purpose, or that it is to be administered as a deterrent to
further sin, or that it is an expression of God's resentment of
an insult offered to his personal dignity.[136] Denying all these
ideas, Dale defines punishment as "the suffering which has been
deserved by past sin."[137] The heart of Dale's argument is that
in Christ, God, who has the moral right to inflict punishment,
has endured it.[138] This, according to Dale, has "all the moral
worth and significance of the act by which the penalties of sin
would have been inflicted on the sinner."[139]

> He did not merely confess our sin. He did not merely acknowl-
> edge that we deserved to suffer. He endured the penalties of
> sin, and so made an actual submission to the authority and
> righteousness of the principle which those penalties express.[140]

Because of Christ's acceptance of the penalties of sin, God can,
without any violation of the eternal law of righteousness or his
own moral character, forgive the sin of man, when by faith man
is united to Christ. Dale terms the concept of the imputation of
sin to Christ a "legal fiction,"[141] and maintains that the atonement becomes ours, not through formal imputation, but by
faith-union with Christ, so that Christ's trust in the Father,
joy in the Father, and love toward the Father become our own.[142]
    One of Dale's most controversial positions is that in the cry
of dereliction from the cross Jesus not only felt himself to be
deserted by God, but he actually was deserted.[143] "He was for-

134 *Ibid.*, p. 64.
135 *Ibid.*, pp. 417-18.
136 *Ibid.*, pp. 432-42.
137 *Ibid.*, p. 435.
138 *Ibid.*, p. 490.
139 *Ibid.*, p. 451.
140 *Ibid.*, p. 481.
141 *Ibid.*, p. 61.
142 *Ibid.*, p. 480.
143 *Ibid.*, pp. 55-60.

saken of God, that we might not have to be forsaken."[144] It is difficult to reconcile this conception with Dale's claim, "There is no schism in the Godhead."[145]

A similar interpretation of the atonement is set forth in the very fine books of the eminent Scottish theologian James Denny: *The Death of Christ* (1902), *The Atonement and the Modern Mind* (1903), and *The Christian Doctrine of Reconciliation* (1917). Though the life of Jesus and his resurrection are not without meaning to Denny, this theologian nevertheless regards the atonement as centering in the death of Christ. "If He had not *died* for us, He would have done nothing at all."[146] Denny maintains that God must forgive in such a way as to demonstrate what he is in relation to sin, a God with whom evil cannot dwell. This is the divine necessity of the death of Christ.[147] Denny declares that the death of Christ is "the ultimate truth about forgiveness; namely, that sin is only forgiven as it is borne."[148]

In *The Cruciality of the Cross* (1909), *The Work of Christ* (1910), and *The Justification of God* (1916) P. T. Forsyth makes significant contributions to the understanding of the atonement along lines similar to those taken by Dale and Denny. Forsyth places special emphasis upon God's holiness, maintaining that it is that which gives stability and moral content to God's love. Defining judgment as "the necessary reaction to sin in a holy God,"[149] Forsyth interprets the cross as the holy God's judgment upon sin. Forsyth and Denny alike emphasize the love of God as the source of the atonement and the unity of the Father and the Son in the atonement. Likewise both theologians maintain that the atonement is not to be explained in quantitative categories, so much punishment borne for so much sin.

Emil Brunner emphasizes the idea that reconciliation is two-

---

[144] *Ibid.*, p. 491.

[145] *Ibid.*, p. 415.

[146] *The Christian Doctrine of Reconciliation* (London: James Clarke & Co., this edition, 1959), p. 274.

[147] *The Death of Christ,* edited by R.V.G. Tasker (London: Tyndale Press, first published in this edition, 1951), p. 187.

[148] *The Christian Doctrine of Reconciliation,* p. 162.

[149] Forsyth, *The Cruciality of the Cross* (New York and London: Hodder & Stoughton, 1909), p. 53.

sided. There is enmity on the side of God as well as on the side
of man.

> God *reconciles,* but He is not reconciled. He *reconciles Himself,*
> but in this process He is only the One who acts, the One who
> gives; He is not also the One who receives.[150]

This is the objective side of the atonement. But there is also a
subjective side. In the Word of divine justification, the objective
and subjective sides meet. "Justification means this miracle:
that Christ takes our place and we take His."[151]

Certainly one of the most profound modern interpretations
of the atonement is that given by Karl Barth in *Church Dogmatics,* IV, 1.[152] The heart of Barth's doctrine is set forth in the
section entitled, "The Judge Judged in Our Place."[153] Man
wants to be his own judge. For this reason God encounters
man in the flesh in the person of his Son and passes on man
"who feels and accepts himself as his own judge the real judgment which he has merited."[154] With strong words Barth emphasizes the substitutionary character of the atonement. "It
came to pass that Jesus Christ, the Son of God, as man, took our
place in order to judge us in this place by allowing Himself to
be judged for us."[155] "In the place of all men he has Himself
wrestled with that which separates them from Him. He has
Himself borne the consequence of this separation to bear it
away."[156] It would seem, however, that Barth pushes the idea
of the transference of sin too far in that he can even speak of
the penitence of Jesus and of his repenting for sinners.[157]

Barth says in the Foreword to IV, 1: "Throughout I have
found myself in an intensive, although for the most part quiet,
debate with Rudolf Bultmann." This is nowhere more evident
than in Barth's strong emphasis upon the objective character of

150 Emil Brunner, *The Mediator,* English translation based on the second
German edition, 1932 (Philadelphia: Westminster Press, 1947), p. 519.
Italics in the original.

151 *Ibid.,* p. 524.

152 (Edinburgh: T. & T. Clark, 1956).

153 *Ibid.,* IV, 1, pp. 211-282.

154 *Ibid.,* IV, 1, p. 220.

155 *Ibid.,* IV, 1, p. 247.

156 *Loc. cit.*

157 *Ibid.,* IV, 1, pp. 260-62.

what happened on Calvary, and that it was a historical event that happened once-for-all.[158]

Perhaps the greatest weakness of Barth's interpretation of the atonement is his tendency to interpret it as efficacious for all, not alone in the sense that he died for all, but in the sense that because he died for all, all will ultimately be saved.

2. *Views of Moral Influence*

Schleiermacher, Ritschl, Bushnell, Rashdall, and Franks are only a few of the theologians who may be mentioned under this category. They all have this in common: they vigorously attack the penal substitution view and maintain that the barrier to reconciliation is on the side of man, not on the side of God.

Friedrich Schleiermacher's great work on systematic theology is *The Christian Faith*.[159] Defining religion in terms of the feeling of absolute dependence, Schleiermacher proceeds to expound the Christian faith in terms of man's God-consciousness. Redemption in Christ is achieved by the power of Christ's God-consciousness in which we come to participate by faith in him as our representative. At points Schleiermacher's view appears to be very close to that of some of the church fathers who seemed to teach atonement by incarnation. Nevertheless, in his emphasis upon the subjective element in the atonement and the effect upon the believer of the love of God in Christ revealed in the cross, Schleiermacher stands in the tradition of Abelard.

> For in His suffering unto death, occasioned by His steadfastness, there is manifested to us an absolutely self-denying love; and in this there is represented to us with perfect vividness the way in which God was in Him to reconcile the world to Himself. . . . [160]

In the *Christian Doctrine of Justification and Reconciliation*[161] Albrecht Ritschl shifts the emphasis away from the offices of Christ to the vocation of Christ. It was in faithfulness to his vocation, the founding of the kingdom of God, which Ritschl virtually equates with the Christian community, that Jesus suffered death. Despite his vigorous denial that the death of Christ is a penal satisfaction, Ritschl nevertheless argues that

---

[158] *Ibid.*, IV, 1, pp. 223, 245, 247.

[159] (Edinburgh: T. & T. Clark, second German edition, 1830, English translation, 1928).

[160] *Ibid.*, p. 458.

[161] (Edinburgh: Edmonston and Douglas, German edition, 1874; English translation, 1900).

it is on the basis of the death of Christ in founding the kingdom of God that God forgives our sins.

Horace Bushnell[162] interprets the cross as the revelation in time of that which is eternal in God. He places great stress upon the sympathy of Christ and his identification with sinners. Bushnell maintains that Jesus bore our sins in the same way that he bore our sicknesses; that is, he bore them on his feelings. "There is a Gethsemane hid in all love, and when the fit occasion comes, no matter how great and how high the subject may be, its heavy groanings will be heard."[163]

Perhaps the most thorough-going Abelardian interpretation of the atonement in the twentieth century is that given by Hastings Rashdall in *The Idea of Atonement in Christian Theology*.[164] Rashdall would reinterpret Peter's words in Acts 4:12 to read something like this:

> There is none other ideal given among men by which we may be saved except the moral ideal which Christ taught by His words, and illustrated by His life and death of love: and there is none other help so great in the attainment of that ideal as the belief in God as He has been revealed in Him who so taught and lived and died.[165]

Rashdall's unorthodox view of the atonement stems perhaps from his unorthodox view of the person of Christ and the Trinity. In all of these positions his interpretation resembles that of Socinus.

R. S. Franks, author of the two-volume work entitled *History of the Doctrine of the Work of Christ* (1918), sets forth his own Abelardian interpretation of the atonement in *The Atonement* (1934). The fundamental problem of the atonement is that of making man forgivable. This is done by creating in the sinner penitence and trust through the revelation of the love of God in the cross. A weakness of Franks' view is the fact that he tries to maintain two contrary principles: that God is love, and that God cannot suffer.

The moral influence view in its emphasis upon the revelation of the love of God in the cross is obviously stating a vital aspect

---

162 *The Vicarious Sacrifice* (New York: Charles Scribner's Sons, 1903, first published, 1866), two volumes.

163 *Ibid.*, Vol. I, p. 47.

164 (New York: The Macmillan Company, first edition, 1919).

165 *Ibid.*, p. 463.

of the atonement; but in denying an objective element in the atonement, the moral influence view, in its various expressions, tends to ignore or distort a vast body of scriptural teaching, and fails to make clear in what sense the death of Christ is a revelation of the love of God.

3. *Views of Vicarious Confession or Vicarious Penitence*

Probably no treatment of the atonement in the modern period has been more influential than that given by the devout Scottish preacher-theologian, J. McLeod Campbell, in his book *The Nature of the Atonement*.[166] Deposed from his church in 1831 because of his teaching that Christ died for all men and that the believer can have the assurance of salvation in Christ, Campbell did not let this embitter him but went on to write one of the most mature treatments of the atonement in Christian history.

Campbell maintains that though Christ suffered for our sins as atoning sacrifice, he did not endure as a substitute the punishment due our sins. Campbell declares:

> The *sufferer suffers* what he suffers *just through seeing sin and sinners with God's eyes, and feeling in reference to them with God's heart.* Is *such* suffering a *punishment?* Is God, in causing such a divine experience in humanity, inflicting a punishment? There can be but one answer.[167]

The answer which Campbell has in mind, of course, is "No!" Just as the tears of a godly parent over a prodigal child are not penal, the sorrow of God over our sins is not penal. But the faith that God so grieves over us is "infinitely more important, as having power to work holiness in us, than the faith that He so punishes. . . ."[168]

Jonathan Edwards had taught that in God's treatment of sin there must be "either an equivalent punishment or an equivalent sorrow and repentance." "An equivalent repentance would be a repentance, humiliation and sorrow proportionable to the majesty despised."[169] Edwards had dismissed the idea of an equivalent repentance as impossible and had proceeded to de-

---

166 (London: James Clarke & Co., fourth edition, 1859; first edition, 1856).

167 *Ibid.*, p. 117. Italics in the original.

168 *Ibid.*, p. 140.

169 Campbell, *op. cit.*, p. 137.

velop the idea of an equivalent punishment for sin. However, Campbell takes Edward's idea of an equivalent repentance and makes it the key to his interpretation of the atonement. The heart of the matter is this:

> That oneness of mind with the Father, which towards man took the form of condemnation of sin, would in the Son's dealings with the Father in relation to our sins, take the form of a perfect confession of our sins. This confession, as to its own nature, must have been a *perfect Amen in humanity to the judgment of God on the sin of man.*[170]

The Son's response to the wrath of God against sin is, "Thou art righteous, O Lord, who judgest so!" This response has all of the elements of a perfect repentance in humanity for all the sin of man — a perfect sorrow, a perfect contrition — all the elements except a personal consciousness of sin. "And by that perfect response in Amen to the mind of God in relation to sin is the wrath of God rightly met, and that is accorded to divine justice which is its due, and could alone satisfy it."[171]

Campbell deals with the atonement both in its retrospective aspect and in its prospective aspect. In its retrospective aspect, the perfect sorrow for sin in humanity expressed by the Son expiates sin and brings peace with God. In its prospective aspect, atonement creates within us the spirit of sonship in relation to the Father of spirits. "The grace of God, which is at once the remission of past sin, and the gift of eternal life, restores to our orphan spirits their Father and to the Father of spirits His lost children."[172] This, of course, presupposes a faith which so unites us to Christ as to produce within us the mind of the Son with relation to sin and the Son's spirit of obedience and sonship in relation to the Father.

Campbell's view is similar to the more refined forms of the penal view in that it recognizes an objective element in the atonement — that the atonement means something to God, that it is the expression of God's righteous judgment upon sin. Yet it differs from the penal view in its insistence that the suffering of the Son is not penal in nature. Campbell's view is also akin to the best of the moral influence views in the emphasis upon the sorrow which arises from sympathy with sinners and identi-

---

170 *Ibid.,* pp. 135-36. Italics in the original.
171 *Ibid.,* p. 137.
172 *Ibid.,* p. 171.

fication with them, and in the emphasis upon the subjective effect of the atonement in producing within us the spirit of sonship. It differs from the moral influence views, however, in that it recognizes an objective element in the atonement.

As commendable as is Campbell's view, it is questionable precisely at its central point. Can one who knows no sin give a perfect confession of man's sin or express a perfect repentance for sin?

Campbell's main line of thought, with variations, of course, is continued by the Anglican scholar, R. C. Moberly, in his book *Atonement and Personality*.[173] Moberly contends that only the sinless can offer the perfect sacrifice of penitence, because this is "impossible to the sinner, just in proportion as it is true that he has sinned."[174] "It is sin, as sin, which blunts the edge, and dims the power of penitence."[175] According to Moberly, the kind of penitence necessary as an atonement for sin "would be possible only to the absolutely sinless."[176] "The perfect sacrifice of penitence in the sinless Christ is the true atoning sacrifice for sin."[177] Campbell had used both the terms "confession of sin," and "repentance" in the sense of contrition or sorrow for sin. Moberly prefers the term "penitence." Certainly "penitence" is a term which is preferable to "repentance," for repentance normally carries the idea of turning from sin; and it is obviously impossible for one to turn from sin if he has never committed sin. Campbell had renounced completely the use of the word "penal" in reference to the sufferings of Christ, but Moberly doubts the wisdom of abandoning the word altogether, and thinks that it is enough to make it clear that there is no thought in the atonement of inflicting or enduring vengeance.[178]

Moberly puts more stress upon the Holy Spirit and upon the church and the sacraments than does Campbell, who had almost completely left these subjects out of the atonement. Moberly declares, "An exposition of atonement which leaves

[173] (London: John Murray, 1924, first edition, 1901).
[174] *Ibid.*, p. 130.
[175] *Ibid.*, p. 43.
[176] *Loc. cit.*
[177] *Ibid.*, p. 130.
[178] *Ibid.*, p. 398.

out Pentecost, leaves the atonement unintelligible — in relation to us."[179]

Moberly's work, however, must not be interpreted simply as a reinterpretation of Campbell. It is a highly original work with a completely independent line of approach. Accordingly, these two together, Moberly and Campbell, present an extremely attractive view of the atonement.

4. *Views of Sacrifice*

Many writers of the modern period have contributed to the understanding of the meaning of sacrifice in the Bible, but perhaps no writers have taken the results of this new understanding and applied them so significantly and successfully to the atonement as have Hicks and Taylor. Since earlier treatments of sacrifice, such as that of Calvin, had assumed that the rationale of sacrifice is propitiation, the new interpretation of sacrifice in men like Hicks and Taylor, which repudiates the idea of propitiation in relation to sacrifice, may be regarded as a new theory of the atonement. In reality it is a rediscovery of an interpretation of sacrifice which finds its fullest explication in the Epistle to the Hebrews.

F. C. N. Hicks' famous work on the subject is *The Fullness of Sacrifice*.[180] Hicks' treatment of the subject is divided into three parts: Part I: The Old Testament and After; Part II: The New Testament; and Part III: After the New Testament. To Hicks the blood of sacrifice stands not for death but for life. "Life — its recovery, uplifting and communication — is the ruling conception of sacrifice. . . ."[181]

> The dedication of human life in perfect obedience was accomplished in Himself as our first-fruits. He offered our human nature which He had made His own. It was accepted; and the Gospels close, as Acts begins, with the transformation which is God's way of accepting what we offer. The body of His humiliation becomes the body of His glory: The material is taken up into the spiritual. . . .[182]

High church ideas about the Lord's Supper appear as Hicks seeks to relate the atonement to the Eucharist. Hicks emphatically denies that there is a repetition of the sacrifice made once-

179 *Ibid.*, p. 151.
180 (London: Macmillan and Company, 1930).
181 *Ibid.*, p. 177.
182 *Ibid.*, p. 176.

for-all upon the cross. Nevertheless, he interprets the Eucharist as "an integral part, for us on earth, of the One Sacrifice in its fullness."[183] Moreover, he affirms that "the Body and Blood of the Eucharist are the Body and Blood of the glorified, not the crucified, Christ."[184]

Vincent Taylor's treatment of the atonement has been set forth in four books: *Jesus and His Sacrifice* (1937), *The Atonement in New Testament Teaching* (first edition, 1940, second edition, 1945), *Forgiveness and Reconciliation* (first edition, 1941, second edition, 1946), and *The Cross of Christ* (1956). The third book deals more with the effects of the atonement than with the atonement itself. The fourth book adds little not found in the other three. The first two books, particularly the first, go to the heart of the matter. Taylor understands the passion sayings in the gospels to mean that Jesus interprets his death as the sacrifice of perfect obedience which he, the Son of Man, must make in fulfilling the mission of the Servant of the Lord. The death of Christ is interpreted as vicarious, representative, and sacrificial. Taylor regards the biblical category of sacrifice as the most adequate one available for explaining the meaning of the atonement. Taylor treats the Old Testament idea of sacrifice as the natural background against which the passion sayings must be understood.

> The aim of sacrifice is the restored fellowship; its medium is a representative offering; its spiritual condition is the attitude of the worshipper; its rationale is the offering of life; its culmination is sharing in the life offered by means of the sacred meal.[185]

The essence of Taylor's view is that Jesus offered the perfect sacrifice of obedience. This offering, when received by faith, becomes the vehicle of the sinner's approach to God. It does not render his obedience unnecessary. Rather it makes it possible.

Taylor's interpretation has much to commend it. However, it is doubtful if this category alone is adequate to express the richness of the meaning of the atonement.

---

183 *Ibid.,* p. 346.
184 *Ibid.,* p. 347.
185 *Jesus and His Sacrifice* (London: Macmillan and Company, 1948), p. 295.

5. *Views of Victory over the Evil Powers*

Attention has already been called to the work of Gustav Aulén in his famous book *Christus Victor* in bringing this category of interpretation to the forefront in modern theology. Aulén regards his view of the victory over the evil powers of sin, death, and the devil achieved through the incarnation, life, death, and resurrection of Jesus as a revival of the "classic" idea of atonement. According to Aulén, in distinction from the Latin view, which regards the atonement as an offering made to God from man's side, the classic view regards the atonement as a continuous divine action, with God remaining throughout the effective agent of redemption. Nevertheless, the drama of redemption has a dualistic background with God in Christ combating and prevailing over the tyrants which hold mankind in bondage. By this victory God becomes reconciled to the world and establishes a new relation between himself and mankind.[186] "God is at once the author and the object of reconciliation: He is reconciled in the act of reconciling the world to Himself."[187] Through the sacrifice of Christ the tyrants are overcome. But these tyrants are the agents of God's judgment on sin. Thus, though the classic view is dualistic, it is not an absolute dualism.

Aulén makes no claim of setting forth a new theory. Rather, he claims to be reformulating the view of the atonement which was dominant in the church for the first thousand years of its history, a view which was recaptured by Luther, but which became obscured again in Lutheran orthodoxy.

Aulén certainly overstates his case, as we have already taken note elsewhere. Victory over the evil powers is undoubtedly one aspect of the biblical witness concerning the atoning work of Christ; but one cannot interpret the whole biblical witness under this category, as Aulén attempts to do, without introducing distortions equally as great as those against which Aulén protests. Nevertheless, the influence of Aulén's work has been great. Sydney Cave,[188] for example, admits that Aulén's work has forced him to rethink his interpretation of the atonement; and though Cave's conclusions are not as narrow as Aulén's, the influence of Aulén upon Cave's thought is easily discernible.

---

186 *Christus Victor,* p. 55.
187 *Ibid.,* p. 56.
188 *Op. cit.,* Preface, p. v.

An emphasis similar to Aulén's, though not necessarily derived from this Swedish theologian, is discernible in such works as Nathaniel Micklem's *The Doctrine of Our Redemption* (1947), Karl Heim's *Jesus der Weltvollender* (1952) and J. S. Whale's *Victor and Victim* (1960).

Chapter Four

Special Problems

I. THE EXTENT OF THE ATONEMENT

Did Christ die for all or only for the elect? If he died for all, does this mean that all will actually be saved? Our position is that the atonement is unlimited in its provision, but limited in its application; that Christ died for all, but that not all will actually be saved.

That Christ died only for the elect, that the atonement is limited in its design only to those who are actually saved, is one of the so-called five points of Calvinism. This is not taught explicitly by Calvin, but it is implicit in Calvin's system. This theological position has been set forth by such men as Francis Turretin, John Owen, Jonathan Edwards, and Charles Hodge. Today, for the most part, this position is held only by the most rigid and ardent Calvinists, among whom may be listed L. Berkhof, Loraine Boettner, and John Murray.

That Christ died for all men but that only believers receive the forgiveness of sins and are saved was one of the five points of Arminianism as set forth in the Remonstrants (1610). This was the position taken by Arminian and Lutheran theologians; and it is, generally speaking, the position held today by all except the strictest Calvinists on the one hand and those who deny eternal punishment on the other. For example, A. H.

Strong, who for the most part adheres to a strong Calvinist position, upholds the Arminian position on this issue.

> The *atonement* is unlimited, — the whole human race might be saved through it; the *application* of the atonement is limited, — only those who repent and believe are actually saved by it.[1]

The real theological basis for the view of limited atonement is the reformed doctrine of election and predestination. If from all eternity God has unconditionally predestined some to salvation and some to damnation, then it follows that Christ could not have died for all men. A secondary basis, though some would regard this as primary also, is an inference from the retributive justice of God and the nature of the punishment which Christ suffered on the cross. Loraine Boettner states it this way:

> If the suffering and death of Christ was ransom for all men rather than for the elect only, then the merits of His work must be communicated to all alike and the penalty of eternal punishment cannot be justly inflicted on any. God would be unjust if He demanded this extreme penalty twice over, first from the substitute and then from the persons themselves. The conclusion then is that the atonement of Christ does not extend to all men but that it is limited to those for whom He stood surety; that is, to those who compose His true Church.[2]

The alternatives posed here are those of universal salvation or limited atonement. Since the idea of universal salvation is obviously to be rejected as *unscriptural,* the alternative which remains is limited atonement.

The view of limited atonement is bolstered by an appeal to the passages of Scripture which speak of Christ giving his life for the church (Eph. 5:25; Acts 20:28), for the sheep (John 10:14-15), or for many (Mark 10:45), to passages which seem to connect election and Christ's work of redemption (Eph. 1: 4, 7; Rom. 8:31-34), and passages which seem to limit the object of Christ's intercessions to the disciples and those whom they would win (John 17:9, 20, 24).

Those who hold the doctrine of limited atonement say that the issue at stake is the purpose of God in the atonement,

---

[1] A. H. Strong, *Systematic Theology* (Philadelphia: Judson Press, 1907, sixteenth printing, 1951), p. 773. Italics in the original.

[2] Loraine Boettner, *The Reformed Doctrine of Predestination* (Grand Rapids, Michigan: Wm. B. Eerdmans Publishing Co., 1951), p. 155.

whether he actually intended to save all or not. Their contention is that the purpose of God cannot be thwarted, and that if
God intended to save all, all would actually be saved.

To those who hold the position of unlimited atonement — that
Christ died for all, but that only those who respond in faith
are saved — the issue centers around the love of God, the scriptural teachings that Christ died for all, the sincerity of the invitation of salvation which goes out to all, and the freedom of
man. How can God be said to love the world, as John 3:16
states that he does, if he sent his Son to die only for the elect?
Or in what sense could it be said that God is not willing that
any should perish, but that all should come to repentance
(II Pet. 3:9), if Christ did not die for all? Are we to suppose
that the elect are the only ones who labor and are heavy laden
and that they are thus the only ones to whom the invitation of
Jesus is issued (Matt. 11:28) or that the elect are the only ones
who are invited to take the water of life without price (Rev. 22:
17)? Do not these very invitations presuppose that the free
response of man, though not meriting salvation, is nevertheless
the condition upon which the benefits of the atonement are
dispensed? Moreover, there are clear assertions in Scripture
that Christ died for all (II Cor. 5:14), that he gave himself a
ransom for all (I Tim. 2:6), that he is the expiation of the sins
of the whole world (I John 2:2; cf. also I Tim. 4:10; Tit. 2:11),
and that he tasted death for every man (Heb. 2:9).

The arguments advanced for a limited atonement are easily
answered. The reformed doctrine of predestination upon which
it is based is a highly questionable one. Moreover, it is an
erroneous interpretation of the atonement which says that if
Christ died for all then the sinner's sins are punished twice if all
are not actually saved. The problem here is that of a quantitative interpretation of sin and punishment, the unjustified
assumption being that there is a quantitative equivalence between the punishment which Christ endured and the sin of
man for which atonement is made.

To say that Christ died for all does not exclude the idea that
he died for the elect and that his death is especially efficacious
in their case. But to say that Christ died only for the elect is
to exclude the idea that he died in any sense for all. The
larger circle includes the smaller one, but the smaller circle
does not include the larger one.

In Galatians 2:20 Paul says that the Son of God "loved me and gave himself for me," but this does not exclude the idea that "Christ loved the church and gave himself up for her" (Eph. 5:25), because he does not say that Christ loved me only and gave himself for me only. For a similar reason, neither does the statement that "Christ loved the church and gave himself up for her" exclude the idea that Christ gave himself a ransom for all (I Tim. 2:6).

Ultimately the question is one of freedom. It is possible for man to resist the Holy Spirit (Acts 7:51), to grieve the Holy Spirit (Eph. 4:30), and even to quench the Holy Spirit (I Thess. 5:19).

II. OBJECTIVE AND SUBJECTIVE ELEMENTS

Generally speaking, the words objective and subjective are used with two different meanings. The first meaning has to do with whether the atonement is an accomplished fact which happened once-for-all in history or whether it is an experience which happens within each individual as by faith he receives the atonement, dying to sin and rising to newness of life. The second meaning has to do with whether the necessity of the atonement is in God or in man, whether it is made with reference to needs that exist primarily in God or primarily in man.

Now the atonement is definitely an objective fact in the first sense of the word. It is a historical fact which occurred once-for-all on a hill called Calvary outside a city called Jerusalem by a man named Jesus around 28-31 A.D. Something happened in history which cannot be repeated, which indeed does not need to be repeated. It is a once-for-all historical event which has universal significance. This is what the New Testament means in the use of the words *eph apax* (Heb. 7:27; 9:12; 10:10) and *hapax* (I Pet. 3:18) with reference to the atonement. Barth states it this way:

> We are dealing with an act which took place on earth, in time and space, which is indissolubly linked with the name of a certain man. . . .
> It is a matter of history. Everything depends upon the fact that this turning as it comes from God for us men is not simply imagined and presented as a true teaching of pious and thoughtful people, but that it happened in this way, in the space and time which are those of all men.[3]

---

[3] Karl Barth, *Church Dogmatics* (Edinburgh: T. & T. Clark, 1956), IV, 1, pp. 245, 247-48.

The atonement is a historical fact. But as long as it remains for me only a historical fact, for me it has no saving significance. The objective atonement must be subjectively appropriated. Moberly states: "An objective fact that is not apprehended in any sense subjectively, is to those who have no subjective relation to it, as if it were non-existent."[4] "It is of necessity that I should be in a certain relation with it: and upon my relation to it its relation to me will ultimately depend."[5] Moberly goes on to point out that the word "subjective" to many people denotes "the hallucinations of a brain diseased, misconceiving untruth as truth."[6] However, when we speak of the subjective appropriation of the atonement, we do not have reference to "the hallucinations of a brain diseased," but to what ought to be the experience of every individual, the acceptance of God's salvation by repentance of sin and faith in Jesus Christ. As Rust puts it: "There can be no atonement unless the objective act on Calvary awakens faith and commitment in sinful man and effects a regeneration of his life."[7]

But these two aspects of the atonement are not to be pulled apart, as if they were independent. It is true that Christ died for my sins whether I recognize it or not or whether by faith I am related to the atonement in a saving way or not. But it is God's purpose that that which is a fact of history should become for me a fact of experience. An overemphasis upon the objective atonement or the finished work of Christ gives the impression that the atonement is automatic and that faith is relatively unimportant.[8] On the other hand, an overemphasis upon the encounter with Christ, upon dying and rising with Christ without a corresponding emphasis upon the once-for-all event of Calvary and the empty tomb, gives the impression that whether Christ actually died for our sins and rose again is irrevelant.[9] Again Moberly perceives the central issue when he states:

> It is first a historical fact, that it may come to be a personal, fact. Calvary, and the Ascension, precede any thought or apprehen-

[4] J. C. Moberly, *The Atonement and Personality* (London: John Murray, 1924, first edition, 1901) , p. 141.

[5] *Loc. cit.*

[6] *Ibid.,* p. 142.

[7] Eric Rust, *Towards a Theological Understanding of History* (New York: Oxford University Press, 1963) , p. 196.

[8] This seems to be the case in Barth's theology.

[9] This seems to be the case in Bultmann's theology.

sion of ours. But Calvary, and the Ascension, are none the less to become an integral part of the experience and reality of our consciousness.[10]

Now the second meaning of the terms objective and subjective with reference to the atonement calls for attention. The satisfaction view of Anselm and the penal substitution view of Calvin are clearly objective in that the necessity of the atonement is primarily on God's side; it is to satisfy the demands of the honor of God or the justice of God. The moral influence view of Abelard and the example view of Socinus, on the other hand, are clearly subjective in that they recognize no barrier to God's forgiving man's sin on the part of God. The only barrier is the impenitence of man, and the purpose of the atonement is through a demonstration of God's love to move man to repent of his sins or to follow the example of Christ in self-sacrifice.

Such subjective views are clearly inadequate because they fail to give expression to the total and inevitable opposition of God to all that opposes his holy will, to the fact that there is a necessity in the divine nature that when sin is forgiven it must be forgiven in such a way as to make the total opposition of God to it unmistakable. Moreover, it is only on the basis of an objective act which has saving significance that God demonstrates his love. In other words, it is by saving us, by performing an act which has saving significance, that God demonstrates his love for us, and not just that God demonstrates his love for us and thus evokes a response from us which results in our salvation.

On the other hand, objective views of the atonement are sometimes stated in such a way as to be unacceptable in that they seem to imply that the purpose of the atonement is to bring about a change in the attitude of God toward the sinner. However, the real purpose of the atonement is to remove the sin-barrier so that God's holy love, which is itself the source of the atonement, may find expression in the salvation of the sinner as he repents of sin and turns in faith to Christ for newness of life.

There is some degree of objectivity in the classic view of Christ's victory over the evil powers, in Grotius' governmental view, and perhaps even in Campbell's view of vicarious confession and Moberly's view of vicarious penitence, and Hicks' and Taylor's view of sacrifice; but the distinction between the

---

10 Moberly, *op. cit.,* p. 143.

objective and subjective elements in these views is not as clear as in the case of the satisfaction and penal substitution views on the one hand, and the moral influence and example views on the other.

The truth of the matter is that the necessity of the atonement is two-sided. On God's part, there is a necessity that forgiveness should be mediated through judgment upon sin. On man's part, there is a necessity for such a demonstration of the seriousness of sin and the depth of God's love as will cause man to repent of sin and turn to Christ for salvation. These two taken together constitute the atonement.

Chapter Five

A Constructive Statement of the Doctrine
of the Atonement

I. PRINCIPLES OF INTERPRETATION

1. The doctrine of the atonement must be based upon and give expression to a worthy concept of the Triune God. It must make it clear that the atonement has its origin in the Triune God himself, that God does not love us because Christ died for us, but that Christ died for us because God loves us, and his sacrifice is an expression of this love. The cross of Christ was not given by man to change God, but given by God to change man. It was the Father who spared not his only Son, but freely gave him up for us all (Rom. 8:32), who loved the world so much that he gave his only Son for its salvation (John 3:16). Far from effecting any change in the attitude of God toward man in the sense of turning hostility into love or making a friend of an enemy, the cross of Christ gave expression to the love of God for man which was in God's heart from all eternity, working out in history God's eternal purpose in Christ.

Though the cross had its origin in the eternal purpose of God, it is, nevertheless, an event in human history, wrought out at a particular time and place, in a particular person. Peter brings the eternal and historical aspects together in a single statement in his sermon on the day of Pentecost: "This Jesus, delivered up according to the definite plan and foreknowledge of God, you crucified and killed by the hands of lawless men . . ." (Acts 2:23). The principle of the cross is clearly stated in Isaiah 63:9 in relation to God's dealings with Israel: "In all their affliction he was afflicted, and the angel of his presence saved them; in his love and in his pity he redeemed them; he lifted them up and carried them all the days of old." "There was a cross in the heart of God before there was one planted on the green hill outside Jerusalem."[1]

No emphasis upon the eternal cross, however, is to be allowed to obscure the significance of the historical fact that the suffering, redeeming love of God did express itself in this way in the context of human history. Though the Epistle to the Hebrews emphasizes the continuing ministry of Christ in the heavenly realm and in this sense expresses the idea of the cross as eternal, no portion of the New Testament places more emphasis upon the once-for-all-ness of the sacrifice of Christ than does this epistle. It is precisely because Christ has made the sacrifice once-for-all that he continues to present the sacrifice to the Father as the basis of our salvation.

Again, the doctrine of the atonement must be stated in such a way as to cast no doubts upon the unity of the Father and the Son. Any view of the atonement which suggests the idea of an angry Father inflicting punishment upon his innocent and loving Son must be rejected as unbiblical. "God was in Christ reconciling the world to himself . . ." (II Cor. 5:19).

Likewise, any view of the atonement which suggests a split in the divine nature, with the love and mercy of God on the one hand being set over against the righteousness and wrath of God on the other, cannot be accepted as satisfactory. God is not a schizophrenic. P. T. Forsyth reminds us that the attributes of God are not things within God which God could handle and adjust. "An attribute of God is God Himself behaving, with all His unity, in a particular way in a particular situation."[2] The love of God is God in his love, and the holiness of God is God in his holiness, and the wrath of God is God in his wrath. Thus the wrath of God and the love of God are not antithetical, as is

1 C. A. Dinsmore, *Atonement in Literature and Life,* p. 232; quoted by D. M. Baillie, *God Was in Christ* (New York: Charles Scribner's Sons, 1948), p. 194.
2 P. T. Forsyth, *The Work of Christ* (London: Hodder and Stoughton, 1910), p. 117.

often supposed. God's wrath is an integral constituent of his love. The wrath of God is the active manifestation of God's essential incapacity to be morally indifferent and let sin alone. It denotes the attitude of God in his love toward wilful sin. "God's wrath is God's grace. It is His grace smitten with dreadful sorrow. It is His love in agony."[3]

In dealing with man's sin problem God acts in such a way as to respect man's freedom. If coercion had been God's method of saving man from sin, the cross would never have become a reality. Indeed, if coercion had been God's method there would have been no need for redemption, for God would not have permitted human sin. In such a case men would have been puppets, mere automatons, obeying their Master because they had no choice. But from such automatons God could have expected no response of love. A puppet can no more love than he can disobey. In the perfect liberty of the Creator God chose to create man as man, with the power of contrary choice. Following the principle of noncoercion, God chose to offer redemption to man in such a way as to attract but not to compel, to appeal but not to coerce. The cross of Christ is the biblical testimony that God acts in a way consistent with his own nature, demonstrating his love while respecting man's freedom. Reconciliation, not revenge, is God's objective. Self-sacrifice, not self-assertion, is his method.

2. The doctrine of the atonement must be based upon and give expression to a correct Christology. It must make it clear that the incarnation is the presupposition of the atonement. Many have suffered death in devotion to duty and truth. In fact, many have died the cruel death of the cross. Jesus was crucified in the midst of two criminals. But that which distinguishes the death of Jesus from the death of a martyr or that of a criminal is the person of the one who was crucified. He was true God and true man. "The word became flesh . . ." (John 1:14). The eternal Christ, existing in the form of God, emptied himself, taking the form of a servant (Phil. 2:6-7). He exchanged heavenly riches for earthly poverty that we might exchange earthly poverty for heavenly riches (II Cor. 8:9). He who was by nature the Son of God became in time the Son of Man, thus eternally uniting humanity to deity in one person.

[3] James Stewart, *A Man in Christ* (New York: Harper and Row), p. 221.

Salvation must come from God. It cannot come from man, for man is a sinner in need of salvation. The very sin of man has shut him off from God and closed the door on all possibilities of an approach to God from man's side. If man is to be saved, God must come to man, because man cannot come to God. Thus the Redeemer must be divine.

But salvation, if it is to be effective, must meet man as he is. It is man of Adam's race who has sinned. Thus sin must be conquered in the sinful race, which is in need of salvation. For this reason the problem of man's sin could not be solved by a divine fiat from above. God had to unite himself to sinful man, that he might unite sinful man unto himself. The Word had to become flesh; the Son of God had to become the Son of Man, within the context of human history.

The incarnation, life, death, and resurrection of Jesus must be treated as a unity and as all essential parts of the saving event of God in Jesus Christ. The life which Jesus lived was a life of perfect obedience to the will of the Father. This is what distinguishes his life from all other human lives. It is doubtful if anything is to be gained by distinguishing between the active obedience of Christ expressed in his life and the passive obedience of Christ as expressed in his death, as it is often done in Calvinistic theology. He was obedient unto death, even the death of the cross (Phil. 2:8). It was the perfect obedience of the Son to the will of the Father which issued in the death of the cross. If at any point Jesus had sinned, if at any point he had been disobedient and had asserted his own will over against the will of the Father, he would himself have been in need of redemption from sin, and would not have been able to confer redemption upon us. The disobedience of the first Adam had to be overcome by the perfect obedience of the second Adam (Rom. 5:18-19; I Cor. 15:45).

In obedience to the will of God revealed to him at his baptism and during the temptations in the wilderness, Jesus accepted for his vocation the fulfilment of the role of the Suffering Servant of Isaiah 53. His mission was that of bringing forth salvation through suffering. It would inevitably involve his being rejected and put to death. The acceptance of this vocation on the part of Jesus, and the steadfast refusal to turn aside to the right or the left, was not an easy thing. It was wrought out in the midst of persistent temptation and inner conflict. He was tempted in all points as we are, yet he did not sin (Heb.

4:15). He accepted his vocation as the cup which he had received from the Father (Mark 10:38; John 18:11), and as the baptism with which he would have to be baptized (Mark 10:38; Luke 12:50). And even when in unspeakable agony he prayed, "My Father, if it be possible let this cup pass from me," this earnest desire which sprang from the depths of his humanity was never allowed to become dominant over his supreme desire, "not as I will, but as thou wilt" (Matt. 26:39). It is this obedience which issued in the cross, which reached its climax in the cross. But this obedience to the will of the Father in the death which he died is meaningless and unintelligible when separated from the life which he lived.

And just as the cross of Christ is not to be separated from the incarnation and life of Jesus on the one hand, neither is it to be separated from the resurrection of Jesus on the other. In the New Testament the death of Christ and the resurrection of Christ are held together in the closest proximity. "For I delivered to you as of first importance what I also received, that Christ died for our sins in accordance with the scriptures, that he was buried, that he was raised on the third day in accordance with the scriptures . . ." (I Cor. 15:3-4). The Lord was "put to death for our trespasses and raised for our justification" (Rom. 4:25).[4] It is the resurrection of Christ which gives saving significance to the death of Christ. "If Christ has not been raised, your faith is futile and you are still in your sins" (I Cor. 15:17). When the disciples looked at the cross from afar, they saw in it only defeat. "But we had hoped that he was the one to redeem Israel" (Luke 24:21). But how could he? He was dead! Following the death of Jesus the disciples were discouraged, defeated, despairing men, meeting behind closed doors for fear of the Jews. Then suddenly a remarkable change took place. These men who had forsaken Jesus and fled, who had been too cowardly to go to the cross with him, now faced those who had put him to death and boldly proclaimed, "You put him to death, but God raised him from the dead!" It was the resurrection of Christ, the appearance of the risen Christ to his disciples, and the coming of the Spirit which wrought this change in the apostles! Apart from the resurrection, the cross is the

4 The close connection between the death and resurrection of Jesus in the biblical witness is indicated by such passages as the following: Matt. 27-28; Mark 15-16; Luke 23-24; John 18-21; Acts 2:23-24; 3:14-15; 4:10; 5:30; 10:39-40; Rom. 6:3-11; 8:34; I Pet. 1:19-21; 3:18, 21-22.

greatest defeat of the ages! Interpreted in the light of the resurrection, the cross is the greatest victory of all time!

Twentieth-century man asks, "How can the crucifixion of a man in the first century have any saving significance for my life today?" Christian faith answers that the one who was crucified in the first century was not just a man, least of all not just a man of the first century. It is the deity of Christ and the resurrection of Christ which make the cross of Jesus the cross of Christ, the power of God unto salvation for everyone who has faith. From a human point of view the crucifixion of Jesus was a heinous crime, but from God's point of view it was the self-giving of divine love. Because the one who was crucified on Calvary nineteen hundred years ago was raised from the dead by the power of God and is alive today, he belongs not just to the first century but to every century. He is our eternal contemporary. And the cross of Christ is eternally relevant to this century and to every century. It is an event in time, but at the same time an event in eternity. Thus the cross of Christ is the inescapable cross!

3. An exposition of the atonement must make it clear that the atonement becomes effective in human experience only through the work of the Holy Spirit. Though the atonement has its origin in the eternal purpose of God, and is wrought out in human history through the work of Jesus Christ, the Son of God, it does not result in salvation for man until the Holy Spirit uses it to evoke a response of repentance and faith, to unite the sinner to the Saviour, who through his incarnation and atoning death has already united himself to the sinner. Moberly[5] has made a significant contribution in relating the work of the Holy Spirit to the atonement. The reality represented by the event of Calvary is objectively realized first that it may be subjectively realized in the experience represented by Pentecost.

> Calvary without Pentecost, would not be an atonement *to us*. But Pentecost could not be without Calvary. Calvary is the possibility of Pentecost: and Pentecost is the realization, in human spirits, of Calvary.[6]

4. An exposition of the atonement must seek to give adequate expression to the great variety of biblical witness concerning the

[5] *The Atonement and Personality* (John Murray, 1924) , pp. 136-255.
[6] *Ibid.*, p. 152. Italics in the original.

subject. Any attempt at compressing the subject into one or two categories must be avoided sedulously. Any such attempt will inevitably result in the distortion which arises from oversimplification, whether it come as the result of ignoring certain important aspects of the biblical witness or as a result of treating diverse elements as one without a due recognition of their diversity. Almost all of the historical views of the atonement give expression to important biblical truths, but many of them fail in their purpose because they seize upon an important aspect of the subject and set it forth as if it were the whole. Certainly this is true in Anselm's view of satisfaction, in Abelard's moral influence view, and in Aulén's Christus Victor view. Even at the risk of a seeming lack of theological precision in the statement of the atonement, the variety of the biblical witness to the meaning of the saving act of God in Jesus Christ must be preserved.

5. We need to recognize with Dale that the fact of the atonement is infinitely more important than any explanation of it. This is not to say that an attempt at theological explanation is unimportant. Rather, it is to underscore the fact we are not saved by subscribing to a certain view of the atonement, but by relying upon the saving act of God in Jesus Christ, however inadequate our understanding may be. Indeed, the subject is so great that there never comes a time when we can tie the whole matter up in one neat theological package without something spilling over.

II. The Meaning of the Cross

We have already called attention to the fact that in the interpretation of the atonement the life, death, and resurrection of Jesus are to be treated as a unity; that is, each part is to be viewed in integral relation to the whole. Nevertheless, in the atonement it is the cross which is central. But the cross of Christ is the cross of the incarnate Son of God, and apart from this fact it would have no saving significance. It is the Son's obedience to the Father which issues in the cross, and the cross is the inevitable and climactic expression of this obedience. The cross of Christ, the cross to which the New Testament bears witness, is the cross interpreted in the light of the resurrection. Bearing in mind the fact that the cross is not to be viewed in isolation from the incarnation, the life of Jesus, and the resurrection, we must, nevertheless, place the emphasis where the New Testament does in the treatment of the atonement; that is, upon the cross of Christ.

1. The cross of Christ is the supreme revelation of the amazing depths of the love of God for sinful man.

The Bible bears witness to other revelations of God's love. The Jews looked upon their redemption from Egypt as a revelation of the love of God. And yet this was an act, which, by its very nature, involved the destruction of one group of people for the salvation of another group. But the cross of Christ has for its aim the salvation of all, even those who crucified Jesus, though when one rejects the cross he is judged as a result.

The love of God was certainly revealed in the history of God's relation to Israel. And yet, in comparison to the love of God revealed in the cross, this love suffers from abstraction and lacks the quality of sacrifice inherent in the giving of God's own Son.

The love of God is marvellously revealed in the life of Jesus, in his teachings, in his deeds of mercy, in his identification with sinners, in his communication of God's forgiveness to those who needed it most; and yet the supreme demonstration is the death of the Son of God upon the cross.

Love is revealed in sacrifice, in vicarious suffering for the object of its love. When a mother sacrifices her life to rescue her child from a burning building, the greatness of her love is thereby manifest. We cannot calculate the intensity of the sufferings of Christ. They were physical, mental, and spiritual. The physical sufferings were perhaps the lightest. A lash was laid upon his back. A crown of thorns was crushed down upon his head. The burden of a heavy cross was laid upon his shoulders. His hands and feet were pierced with nails. His tongue clave to the roof of his mouth as he experienced the agonies of intense thirst, and his whole body cried out from the pain of exhaustion.

His mental agony included his deep sorrow over the failure of his people to repent, the experience of their ingratitude, and the insults and mockery to which he was subjected.

But the deepest, and certainly the most incalculable aspect of our Lord's suffering, was the spiritual. He who knew no sin had become completely identified with sinners. He who because he was sinless was not supposed to die — for death is the wages of sin — was not only submitting to death but to the death of the cross, perhaps the most painful, and certainly the most shameful of all deaths. So intense was his spiritual suffering that it brought forth from the depths of his soul the agonized cry, "My God, my God, why hast thou forsaken me?" (Mark 15:34).

The cross of Christ reveals the amazing depths of the love of God for sinful men because it was directed towards those who were completely unworthy of it. Human sacrifice is conditioned by the worthiness of the object for which it is made. Paul says that for a righteous man, a stern model of duty, one would hardly die. Yet for a good man, a man rich in love and mercy, a paragon of kindness, one might willingly give his life (Rom. 5:7). And yet the amazing thing about Christ's love is that he did not die for those who were righteous or good, but for those who were sinners (Rom. 5:8). Paul uses four strong words to emphasize the unworthiness of the objects of Christ's love. Christ died for us when we were helpless, ungodly, sinners, and enemies (Rom. 5:6, 8, 10).[7] This means that God did not wait for us to become good or for us to turn from our sins, but while we were yet in rebellion against him, God loved us and proved his love for us in giving his Son to die for us (Rom. 5:8; 8:32). A similar teaching is found in I John 4:9-10, where John says that love has its origin in God, not in man. Here John treats not only the cross, but the incarnation as well, as a manifestation of the love of God. Twice John says, "God sent his son." He sent his Son to be the expiation of our sins that we might live through him. This emphasis is similar to that of John 3:16-17, where the sending of the Son and the giving of the Son refer to the whole saving act of God in Jesus Christ. This passage makes it clear that the incarnation and the atonement have their origin in God's great love for the world.

The love revealed in the cross is the love both of the Son and of the Father. It is the love of the Son, because the Son freely gave himself (John 10:17-18; Eph. 5:2, 25; II Cor. 5:14). But it is also the love of the Father, because it is the Father "who did not spare his own Son but gave him up for us all . . ." (Rom. 8:32; cf. John 3:16; I John 4:9-10). Indeed in Romans 5:8, where we would expect Paul to say that Christ shows his love for us by dying for us while we were yet sinners, he says, "But

---

[7] Cf. Anders Nygren, *Agape and Eros* (London: S.P.C.K., 1932), Vol. I, pp. 52-56.

God shows his love for us." Here the reflexive pronoun *heautou* is used for emphasis, and the meaning is that God shows his *own* love.

No appeal has such power to melt hardened hearts and move us to repentance and trust as the love of God revealed in the death of Christ. This is the great truth of the moral influence theory, the undeniable subjective element in the atonement.

And yet this view cannot stand alone, as the exponents of the moral influence view would sometimes try to lead us to think. We can see the love of God revealed in the death of Christ for us only if that death is related in some objective way to our salvation from sin. We must not forget that Romans 3:25-26 comes before Romans 5:8 and I John 2:2 comes before I John 4:9-10. It is because Christ in his death removes the barrier between us and God and thereby opens the way of salvation for us that we can see the love of God for us manifested in his cross. Therefore, for a proper understanding of this aspect of the atonement, we must have some understanding of the objective side of the atonement as well.

2. The cross of Christ is God's judgment upon man's sin.

Paul declares, "For God has done what the law, weakened by the flesh could not do: sending his own Son in the likeness of sinful flesh and for sin, he condemned sin in the flesh" (Rom. 8:3). Salvation is mediated through judgment. This is a principle which answers to a necessity which exists both in the nature of God and in the nature of man. In the nature of God there is a necessity that forgiveness of sin should be mediated in such a way as to disclose unmistakably the mind of God toward sin, and thereby manifest his utter revulsion to it. God is inexorably opposed to all that stands in opposition to his own holy will. In the nature of man there is the necessity that, if forgiveness is to be true salvation, it should be mediated in such a way as to produce in man the mind of God toward sin. This can be done only if the utter seriousness of man's sin and the dreadful costliness of forgiveness is disclosed. The judgment of God upon sin in the cross answers to this necessity which exists in the nature of God and in the nature of man.

That salvation is mediated through a decisive judgment of God upon sin is Paul's emphasis in Romans 3:24-26. An illustration of this principle is to be found in the use which John makes of the narrative in the Old Testament concerning the lifting up

of the serpent in the wilderness (Num. 21:4-9; John 3:14-15).
The fiery serpents in the wilderness were the instruments of God's
judgment upon the sin of Israel. And yet salvation came as the
Israelites accepted the method of salvation which God had appointed and looked upon a fiery serpent which Moses had made
out of bronze and placed upon a pole. The serpent, which had
been the medium of God's judgment, now became God's appointed medium of salvation. The cross of Christ is God's own
judgment upon sin, but it is also God's appointed means of
salvation for sinful man. The idea of necessity expressed in
John 3:14-15 seems to be that of the necessity that salvation
should come through judgment.

H. R. Mackintosh[8] discusses three ways in which man's sin
is judged in the cross of Christ, and we can do no better than
follow his outline.

First, says Mackintosh, "Sin is condemned in the cross because
it there is permitted fully to expose its true nature."[9] In Jesus
for the first time mankind was confronted with perfect goodness
and perfect love. Thus in man's treatment of Jesus, sin's malev-
olent antagonism to perfect love was revealed for the first time
without reserve and its evil laid bare to the bone.[10]

The nature of the sacrifice reveals the seriousness of man's
sin. It was to save man from sin that God sent his Son into the
world and that he delivered him up to death. Surely, if sin
had not been a horribly dreadful reality, God would not have
chosen such a drastic way of providing a way of salvation from
it. Just as the degree of power needed to move a huge rock from
the road is the measure of the weight of the rock, even so the
degree of sacrifice needed to save man from sin is the measure of
the exceeding greatness of man's sin.[11]

It has frequently been pointed out that the human instruments of history's most heinous sin were the Jewish religious
leaders and representatives of the Roman government. The
Jewish religion was unquestionably the highest form of religion
that had appeared until that time; yet the religious leaders of
the Jews, out of what they regarded as zeal for their faith, in-

[8] The Christian Experience of Forgiveness (London: Nisbet & Co., first
published, 1927), pp. 198-206. While the three-point outline is Mackintosh's, the discussion given here, unless otherwise indicated, is my own.
[9] Ibid., p. 198.
[10] Loc. cit.
[11] Cf. Emil Brunner, Our Faith (London: SCM Press, 1950), pp. 43-44.

stigated the death of Jesus. The Roman government's great contribution to the world was civil law. This government prided itself on the justice of its courts. And yet it was a Roman governor, who, after three times having declared Christ innocent, condemned him to death; and the sentence was carried out by soldiers of Imperial Rome. This seems to suggest that that which springs from man, even his best, is filled with sin throughout.

But we do not truly understand the cross as a revelation of the dreadful seriousness of man's sin until we realize that the sins which crucified Jesus were not just the sins of the Jewish religious leaders and the Roman officials of that day. They were our sins. It was envy and jealousy such as is present in our lives which led the Jewish religious leaders to instigate the death of Jesus. The lust for power and material gain led Judas to betray his Lord, and moral cowardice led Peter to deny Jesus and Pilate to condemn him to death. All of these are our sins. When given a choice between Jesus and Barabbas, the crowds chose Jesus to be crucified and Barabbas to be released. Even so, we, when faced with choices between good and evil, often choose the evil instead of the good. Ultimately the problem was the rebellion of the creature against its Creator, man's desire to push God out of his world and govern his own life without any interference from God. "It is like the wicked husbandmen who behave as if God's vineyard were their own and kill the heir when He comes for the fruits."[12] "The fact that God gave Christ to men, and they could do no better than crucify Him, casts a terrible light upon our nature."[13]

The cross reveals to us the dreadful horror of our sins. And it is only when we see sin in its true light that we cast ourselves upon the mercy of God with the prayer, "God, be merciful to me a sinner!" (Luke 18:13).

Second, as Mackintosh says, "Sin is judged in the cross by Jesus' attitude to its intrinsic evil."[14] It is human nature to seek the easy way. The instinct for self-preservation asserts itself, and we readily turn to the right or the left to avoid an unpleasant situation or to pursue a selfish advantage. Expediency takes the place of principle; compromise is interpreted as di-

[12] Leslie Newbigin, *Sin and Salvation* (London: SCM Press, 1956), p. 75.
[13] Mackintosh, *op. cit.*, p. 199.
[14] *Loc. cit.*

plomacy; and social acceptability as manifested by universality of practice (everybody does it) becomes the standard for judging right and wrong. After all life does not face us with clearcut choices between good and evil, we say. In a world like this compromise is the law of survival. But Jesus did not interpret the meaning of life in terms of survival but in terms of doing the will of God. He revealed his utter antagonism to sin, not just through words denouncing its evil, but by a steadfast refusal to compromise with sin, even when to pursue such a course meant to suffer death at the hands of sinners. The author of Hebrews writes, "In your struggle against sin you have not yet resisted to the point of shedding your blood" (Heb. 12:4). But Jesus did resist sin to the point of shedding blood, not of shedding the blood of others, but of permitting his own blood to be shed. In the light of his cross our appeals to expediency, diplomacy, and social acceptability are seen for what they are — inept attempts at self-deception, moral cowardice seeking to veil its sin in a cloak of respectability.

Third, and this is the crucial point, "Sin is judged in the cross of Jesus because the connexion between sin and suffering is there made utterly clear."[15] Perhaps this is the most strongly emphasized and the most frequently misunderstood aspect of the atonement. That the cross involves some kind of connection between sin and suffering is emphasized by such passages of Scripture as Mark 10:45; Romans 3:25-26; 5:8; 8:3; I Corinthians 15:3; II Corinthians 5:14-15, 21; Galatians 1:4; 3:13; I Timothy 2:5-6; I Peter 1:18-21; 2:24-25; 3:18.

The Bible says that Christ bore our sins (I Pet. 2:24; cf. Isa. 53:4-6). Concerning our need to have Christ bear our sins Barth says:

> All sin, great or small, flagrant or less obvious, needed and needs to have been and to be borne by Him. When He bears it, even the greatest of sins cannot damn a man. If it were not that He bears it, even the smallest would be enough to damn him utterly.[16]

But how does Christ bear our sins? Barth[17] speaks of the judge as judged in our place, and Dale[18] asserts that in Christ

---

15 *Ibid.*, p. 202.

16 Karl Barth, *Church Dogmatics* (Edinburgh: T. & T. Clark, 1965), IV, 1, p. 405.

17 *Ibid.*, IV, 1, pp. 211-82.

18 R. W. Dale, *The Atonement* (London: Congregational Union of England and Wales, first edition, 1878, twenty-sixth edition, 1914), p. 490.

God, who has the moral right of inflicting penalty for sin, has endured the penalty instead of inflicting it. Both of these statements are biblical and both are true. And yet we do not grasp the atonement in its most vital aspect until we go beyond the categories of law to interpret the atonement in terms of Christ's sympathetic identification with sinners. The reason is that we are not dealing with abstract entities such as law or justice or punishment or even love, but with personal relations — God's relation to man and man's relation to God.

That sin entails pain has been written into the constitution of things by the Creator of the universe. But human beings live their lives in such inextricably close connections with others that the evil consequences of sin do not always fall most severely on the guilty. Though the guilty are injured in character and estranged from God, nevertheless, it frequently happens that the greater part of the evil resulting from their sin may fall upon the innocent whose lives are closely entwined with theirs.[19]

In our discussion of the New Testament witness concerning the atonement we have already called attention to Jesus' identification with sinners, of his making their lot his own, of his acceptance of the role of the Suffering Servant. This began at his baptism, continued throughout his ministry, and reached its climax in the cross where he was literally numbered with the transgressors, being crucified between two guilty criminals.

Mackintosh aptly says:

> It was not that God stretched His hand from the sky, seized the mass of human iniquity, transferred it to Jesus by capricious fiat, then chastised Him for it. God does nothing in that way. But when Jesus entered into our life, took the responsibility of our evil upon Himself, identifying His life with ours to the uttermost and placing Himself where the sinful are by strong sympathy in a fashion so real that the pain and affliction due to us became unspeakable suffering within His soul — *that* was the act of God. . . .[20]

We may state the principle of identification with reference to the atoning work of God in Christ as follows. First, by incarnation, through which he became one with the race, and by sympathetic identification with sinners, the Son of God made the lot of sinful, suffering humanity his own. Second, because

---

19 Mackintosh, *op. cit.,* p. 203.
20 *Ibid.,* p. 205. Italics in the original.

of his oneness with the Father, who is holy love, and because of his identification with sinners so completely that he felt the burden of their sin as though it had been his own, there was within the experience of Jesus a creative tension of unimaginable intensity. The record of Jesus' prayer in Gethsemane and his cry of dereliction from the cross give us only a hint of the terrible spiritual struggle which he experienced. Third, this tension came in the form of his acceptance in his own person of the divine judgment on sin. "For the very reason that he was related to the sinful with such profound intimacy, the judgment of God on their sin struck *him*. . . ."[21] Because of his perfect holiness Jesus knew the horror of sin in a way that sinful man, for the very reason that his heart has been contaminated and his conscience seared by sin, could never know. While not ceasing to identify himself with the sinner, he expressed in his life the dreadful seriousness of sin as seen from God's side. Accepting the judgment which holiness necessarily passes upon sin, Christ "confesses that judgment to be holy from amid the deepest experience of it; the experience not of a spectator but of a participant."[22] Fourth, through his identification with sinners and his submitting to God's judgment upon sin, he makes an appeal to our hearts which the Holy Spirit can use to cause us to turn from our sins and identify ourselves with him by faith.

Christ, the sinless one, so identified himself with us in our sin that he experienced its shame and horror and the suffering which sin entails as though the sin had been his own. This is probably the way in which II Corinthians 5:21 should be interpreted. "For our sake he made him to be sin who knew no sin, so that in him we might become the righteousness of God." Our becoming the righteousness of God does not come about in any mechanical or strictly forensic way, but in a vital way, as his identification with us in our sin leads us to identify ourselves with him in his righteousness. That this is the correct interpretation of Paul is indicated by what Paul says earlier in the same chapter (verses 14-15). The love of Christ constrains us because of a certain interpretation which we place on the death of Christ. We judge it to mean that one has died for

<hr/>

21 *Ibid.*, p. 204.

22 J. S. Whale, *Victor and Victim* (Cambridge University Press, 1960), p. 76.

all, and therefore that he has died the death of all. It is the realization that he died the death we should have died which causes us to feel the strong appeal of Christ's love and no longer live for ourselves but for him who died for us and rose again. In the judgment on sin in the cross, by which God vindicates his own righteousness, he makes us righteous, when we accept Christ by faith (Rom. 3:24-26). In the act by which God judged man's sin in the death of his Son, God makes it possible for us to fulfill the just requirements of the law as we walk not according to the flesh but according to the Spirit (Rom. 8:3-4). A similar emphasis is found in I Peter 2:24 where it is said that Christ bore our sins in his own body on the tree, "that we might die to sin and live to righteousness."

Thus we see that the principle of identification works two ways. In divine love Jesus identified himself with us in our sin, bearing the shame, suffering, and death, which we, not he, deserved. But Christ's death for us has redemptive significance in our lives only when it leads us by faith to identify ourselves with him in his way of life so that we may say with Paul: "I have been crucified with Christ; it is no longer I who live, but Christ who lives in me; and the life I now live in the flesh I live by faith in the Son of God, who loved me and gave himself for me" (Gal. 2:20).

3. The Christ-event is God's decisive action by which we are delivered from all the evil powers which hold us in bondage: sin, the law, death, and the devil.

Here it is impossible to think simply of the cross, even when we remember that we are dealing with the cross of the incarnate Son of God and that we are interpreting that cross in the light of the resurrection. The whole Christ-event — incarnation, life, death, and resurrection — is God's mighty action for man's salvation, through which a decisive victory has been won, through which a new situation is created. Christ, the mighty warrior, has pitted his strength against all of the mighty powers which have held us in bondage, and he has won the decisive victory. The enemy that we face is not now unbeaten and unbeatable. He has already been defeated. Christ has defeated all of the evil powers, and he has defeated them as our representative. The victory is ours when by faith we are united to him.

Gustav Aulén, who probably has done more than any other theologian to bring this point of view to the fore in the theological world today, states the point in this way:

The background is the divine will and the forces opposed to it. Christ stands as the warrior and victor of the divine will in the struggle against the evil powers in every form. The antagonism between the divine will and evil comes to a focus in a decisive conflict. The evil powers appear to have won the victory. But Christ wins the victory in apparent defeat and triumphs in his death. Divine love is victorious in self-giving and sacrifice. This decisive victory creates a new situation and changes the estate of both man and the world. A new age has begun. The finished work signifies the victorious coming of divine love. Christian faith is born with a paean of praise in its heart: 'In all this we are more than conquerors,' no power whatsoever 'shall be able to separate us from the love of God, which is in Christ Jesus our Lord' (Rom. 8:37ff.; cf. also 'Thanks be to God, who giveth us the victory through our Lord Jesus Christ,' I Cor. 15:57) .[23]

a. Christ has won the victory over sin, and in this victory we participate by faith. He has faced every temptation that is common to man and has emerged victorious. Through the victory of Christ, man, who is the slave of sin (John 8:34; Rom. 6:16) , is delivered from its bondage. Man in his sin put to death the Son of God, but God in his mercy used this epitome of man's rebellion against his Creator to open up a way of salvation for sinful man.

In Romans 5:12-21 Paul treats Christ as the second Adam who recovers for man all that was lost through the first Adam. Through the first Adam sin entered the world, and death as the penalty of sin. Moreover, death passed to all men because all sinned. Adam's sin was disobedience, and this is the sin of every son of Adam. But the second Adam, Christ, countered Adam's disobedience with perfect obedience. As the disobedience of one man involved all men in condemnation, the obedience of one man results in the free gift of justification for all.

Paul doubtless thought of Adam as a single historical personality. Whether we regard him so or not, the principle remains the same. Just as there is a racial solidarity in man's sin, there is a racial solidarity in God's provision for our salvation.

The early church fathers liked to use the story of David's victory over Goliath to illustrate this point. By David's victory over Goliath, the arch-enemy, the whole army of the Philistines was routed, and the Israelites participated in the victory.

Ultimately, however, this view cannot stand alone. It demands the presupposition that in Christ our sin has been judged and that he has accepted our responsibility for sin as his own. The objective power of guilt is real, and we can be victorious over the tempter only when we realize that our sin has been covered, that Christ has made our responsibility for sin his own.

b. Christ has delivered us from the law. The bond of legal demands, to use Paul's graphic language, has been nailed to the cross (Col. 2:14; cf. Rom. 10:4; Gal. 3:13; 5:1). Our salvation rests upon a different principle than salvation through the works of the law or self-effort. It is grounded in faith in Christ (Gal. 2:16).

c. Christ has won the victory over death. He has been raised from the dead by the power of God. He has triumphed over the grave, because it was impossible for the grave to hold him. The resurrection of Christ is the ground of the believer's hope of resurrection. "Now in fact Christ has been raised from the dead, the first fruits of those who have fallen asleep" (I Cor. 15:20). Death still remains as a physical phenomenon, but it has been destroyed in principle (II Tim. 1:10), because its meaning has been changed. It has been swallowed up in victory, because it has lost its sting. The sting of death is sin, the objective power of guilt, the bad conscience. Sin finds its strength in the law, which gives a knowledge of sin, but which does not give power to overcome it. But the sting of sin and the power of sin have been removed because Christ redeems us from sin and from the dominion of the law. Thus we can shout the triumph song, "But thanks be to God, who gives us the victory through our Lord Jesus Christ" (I Cor. 15:57; cf. 15:55-56). The victory that Christ has already won over death is the basis of our confidence that he will win the final victory, and that in the end death itself shall be destroyed (I Cor. 15:26).

d. Christ has won a decisive victory over the devil and all demonic powers. The biblical drama of redemption is set against a dualistic background. There are spiritual powers in the unseen world which are inimical to God. And yet the dualism is not an absolute one. There is only one absolute power, and that is God. Though the devil and his subordinates are in rebellion against God, God permits their existence because they are the executors of his wrath. Luther expresses this idea by describing the devil as God's devil, and the works of the devil as the works of God's left hand. Moreover, the complete and final overthrow of the devil is assured.

Against such a dualistic background the New Testament views Christ's work of redemption. "The whole world is in the power of the evil one" (I John 5:19). "The reason the Son of God appeared was to destroy the works of the devil" (I John 3:8). Satan assaulted Jesus in the wilderness, but Jesus was victorious over the tempter (Matt. 4:1-11; Luke 4:1-13). Jesus is the one stronger than Satan, who enters the strong man's house and spoils his goods (Mark 3:27). His miracles of exorcising evil spirits are a sign that the kingdom of God has come (Matt. 12:28 = Luke 11:20). Jesus interprets the victory of the seventy over the evil spirits as a sign that Satan has fallen from heaven (Luke 10:18). Jesus sees the contest with the evil powers as coming to its climax in the cross; and when his enemies come to take him he says to them, "When I was with you day after day in the temple, you did not lay hands on me. But this is your hour, and the power of darkness" (Luke 22:53).

Had the rulers of this world (meaning the evil spiritual powers, or the evil spiritual powers standing behind the religious and political leaders who were the instruments of the crucifixion) understood the wisdom of God, they would never have crucified the Lord of glory (I Cor. 2:8). The cross is the supreme instrument which God has used in their overthrow (Col. 2:14-15). These powers did not know that God was going to raise Jesus from the dead and use the cross to draw men from the dominion of Satan to the dominion of God, like a magnet draws iron filings to itself (John 12:31-33). The writer of Hebrews says that Jesus shared our nature, that by death he might destroy the one who has the power of death and deliver all those who through fear of death were subject to lifelong bondage (Heb. 2:14-15).

Christ's victory is real, and yet it is not yet complete. We live our lives in a state of tension between the "already" and the "not yet." Christ has already come, the kingdom is already a reality, the age of fulfilment has already dawned. And yet Christ is yet to come, God's reign has not yet been perfected, and the age to come is yet in the future. Christ has already conquered sin, and we have already died with Christ. And yet, the struggle with the old nature continues, and we must daily crucify the flesh with its passions and lusts. Christ has already conquered death; we already have eternal life. And yet death still remains as a fact of human experience, and we must live in hope looking for the final abolition of death (I Cor. 15:26). Christ has already won the decisive victory over the devil, and he has already delivered us from his power. And yet the devil still goes about like a roaring lion seeking victims to devour (I Pet. 5:8). Since the devil's final overthrow will not be consummated until the *eschaton* (I Cor. 15:24-25; Rev. 20:10), we still need the whole armor of God to be able to stand against his wiles (Eph. 6:10-18).

Nevertheless, the victory which Christ has already won is the solid basis for the hope of the ultimate victory which he will yet win. And the victory which he has won he has won as our representative, on our behalf. By faith we now share in the fruits of this victory, and by faith we shall share in the ultimate victory, which Christ is yet to win.

The victory which Christ has already won is on a cosmic scale (Col. 1:20), and the victory which he shall yet win will be greater still (Rom. 8:18-23). At the *eschaton* the harmony within nature which has been disrupted by the fall will be restored, and our bodies will be redeemed from corruption.

The doctrine of the atonement is the Christian affirmation that God has taken life's worst and brought forth life's best. The forces of evil hurled their worst at Christ. In the Christ-event — the incarnation, life, death, and resurrection of Jesus — God took the nadir of human and demonic evil and brought forth the epitome of divine good. This is the victory which God in Christ has won once-for-all and which he offers to all who are united to Christ by faith — salvation out of sin, life out of death, hope out of despair. A God who can do this is not the helpless victim of circumstances beyond his control, but he is the Lord of history, the Master of life and death. Once the believer has apprehended the victory that God in Christ has won, his voice rises with that of Paul in a paean of praise to God: "If God be for us, who can be against us" (Rom. 8:31, King James Version)? "But thanks be to God, who gives us the victory through our Lord Jesus Christ" (I Cor. 15:57).

4. Christ as our high priest makes the perfect representative sacrifice for sin, through which our sins are covered and through which we can make our approach to the holy God. This means that the victor is also the sacrificial victim.

Man ought to render to God the sacrifice of perfect obedience.

Since God is holy, this is what God requires. If man always rendered to God the sacrifice of perfect obedience, no other sacrifice would be necessary. But this is what man does not do. Indeed, this is what he cannot do for the very reason that he is a sinner and thus the slave of sin.

In the Old Testament there is the recognition of this problem, and the sacrificial system is given as at least a partial solution. The sacrifices were not offered to secure God's favor, for the provision of sacrificial worship itself was God's gift and an evidence of his grace. Though sacrifice in the ancient world was often an attempt on the part of man to placate an angry deity, this is not the understanding of sacrifice which Old Testament religion reflects. In the Old Testament, as we have already seen, the purpose of sacrifice was not that of placating an angry god but of covering man's sin and providing a means of approach to a holy God.

> The real intention of the old sacrifices for sin was that the blood of an unblemished victim, representing a stainless life offered to God in death, might be applied so as to remove defilements caused by sin, in order that man might draw near to God in worship, and communion between man and God be established.[24]

Whale points out that Jesus, by blending the Old Testament figures of the Son of Man and Suffering Servant, did something for Old Testament interpretation which had never been done before. Whereas the Son of Man in the Old Testament is a triumphant figure, in the gospels Jesus portrays him as a figure of sacrifice. "The Victor of the Old Testament tradition is both Victor and Victim in the New."[25] Whale goes on to say that in speaking of his body as being broken and his blood as being shed for many, Jesus was interpreting "his redeeming work on the Cross as a sacrificial offering to the Father, made representatively, on behalf of all humanity."[26]

It is the author of Hebrews who, more than any other writer in the New Testament, interprets the atonement in terms of sacrifice. He sees the main value of the sacrifices of the Old Testament system in the fact that, imperfect as they were, they nevertheless foreshadowed the perfect sacrifice offered in Christ

[24] Oliver Chase Quick, *Doctrines of the Creed* (London: Nisbet & Co., 1954), p. 233.
[25] Whale, *op. cit.*, p. 44.
[26] *Loc. cit.*

(Heb. 10:1). The Old Testament priesthood and the Old Testament sacrifices were imperfect (Heb. 7:23-24; 10:4); but Christ, our eternal high priest, through one sacrifice, the sacrifice of himself, has secured eternal redemption (Heb. 10:11-14).

The victim of the Jewish sacrificial ritual was supposed to be an animal without spot or blemish. Only that which was without spot or blemish was worthy to be offered to God. But the purity of this sacrificial victim was physical and ritual. Christ is our sacrificial victim, a lamb without spot or blemish (I Pet. 1:19); but his purity is moral and spiritual. The sacrificial animal in the Old Testament was the unconscious and unwilling victim. But Jesus has consciously and willingly offered himself to God on our behalf (John 10:17-18; Eph. 5:2). Because of the passive and nonmoral nature of the Old Testament sacrifice, the blood of sacrifice, at best, was effective only for ritualistic cleansing (Heb. 9:13; 10:4), whereas the blood of Christ, who through the eternal Spirit offered himself without blemish to God, is efficacious to purify the conscience from dead works to serve the true and living God (Heb. 9:14).

In the Old Testament ritual of sacrifice the worshipper placed both hands upon the head of the sacrificial victim (Lev. 1:4; 3:2; 3:8, 13; 4:4). This seems to have symbolized the offerer's identification of himself with the sacrificial animal: "and it shall be accepted for him to make atonement for him" (Lev. 1:4). What happened thereafter to the victim happened symbolically to the worshipper. By faith we identify ourselves with Christ, who made the perfect sacrifice on our behalf. His sacrifice for our sins becomes effective for us only when we participate in it by faith.

In the Old Testament ritual the victim was slain by the worshipper. It was our sins which crucified Jesus, as we have already taken note. Following the slaying of the victim by the worshipper, the most important part of the ritual was the manipulation of the blood by the priest or the high priest. In the Old Testament system the priest and the sacrifice were different; but in the sacrifice which Christ offered, Christ himself is both the sacrifice which is made and the high priest who offers it. The Old Testament high priests were qualified for their service only through sympathetic identification with the people and by divine appointment (Heb. 5:1-4). Christ meets both of these requirements, but in a way which far surpasses the Old Testament high priests. The high priests of the old dispensation had to offer sacrifices for their own sins, because they themselves were sinners (Heb. 5:3). Now because Christ was tempted at all points like we are, he is able to sympathize with us in our weaknesses (Heb. 4:15); but because he was without sin, he had no need to offer sacrifices on his own behalf. Moreover, Christ was made a high priest for us by divine appointment (Heb. 5: 5-6); and unlike the high priests of the old dispensation, who because of death were unable to continue their service, Christ is forever our high priest by the power of an indestructible life (Heb. 7:16).

Following the slaying of the victim by the worshipper, the Old Testament high priest took the blood of the victim into the holy place and sprinkled it upon the altar, or if it was the Day of Atonement, into the Holy of Holies and sprinkled it upon the mercy seat. The idea was that of taking the blood as far as possible into the presence of God. But Christ, following the offering of himself, has not entered a sanctuary made with hands, but through his resurrection and ascension has passed into heaven to appear before God on our behalf (Heb. 9:24).

The blood is the symbol of the life. By pouring the blood upon the altar or upon the mercy seat the high priest symbolized the dedication of the worshipper to God. Jesus through his obedience unto death made the perfect offering of himself to God, expressing through the laying down of his life in death the principle by which he lived: "Lo, I have come to do thy will" (Heb. 10:9; cf. Psa. 40:7-8). Because of the perfectness of his obedience, because Christ is the lamb without spot or blemish, his sacrifice is received by God. But because our lives are polluted by sin we dare not offer ourselves as we are to God. But when by faith we identify ourselves with his perfect sacrifice on our behalf, then our imperfect obedience is taken up into his perfect obedience and covered by it, and our offering of ourselves is accepted by the holy God. Christ's offering of himself does not make our sacrifice of self unnecessary. Rather it is his sacrifice on our behalf which makes our offering possible.

The Old Testament high priests were continually offering the same sacrifices to God. In this there was the recognition that the sacrifices were inadequate to accomplish the purpose for which they were designed (Heb. 10:1-2). But Christ has once-for-all offered himself, and thereby accomplished eternal redemption (Heb. 10:11-14). The sacrifice does not need to be repeated. Indeed the sacrifice is of such a nature that it cannot be repeated.

The sacrifice is both given by God and offered to God. It is both God's movement to man and the vehicle of man's movement to God. It brings God to man that man might be brought to God. It is given by God, because God has given Christ to be our high priest and our sacrifice, because it is the Father who did not spare his only Son but gave him up freely for us all (Rom. 8:32; cf. Gen. 22:8). It is the gift of his grace. But the sacrifice is also offered to God, and it is offered to God on man's behalf. "Christ loved us and gave himself up for us, a fragrant offering and sacrifice to God" (Eph. 5:2). Christ, through the eternal Spirit, offered himself without blemish to God that he might purify our hearts from dead works to serve the true and living God (Heb. 9:14). And the purpose for which Christ gave his life is accomplished when we make his sacrifice the vehicle of our approach to God and by faith-union with him die to sin and rise to newness of life.

But Christ as our high priest not only gave himself once-for-all as the sacrifice for our sins. He continues a ministry of intercession on our behalf. He not only saves us; he keeps us saved. He has entered into the heavens, there to appear before God on our behalf (Acts 5:30-31; Rom. 8:34; Heb. 4:14-16; 6: 19-20; 7:23-25; 9:24; 10:19-25; I John 2:2). While he was here in the flesh, Jesus interceded for his disciples (Luke 22:31-32; John 17). Now he is continuing that ministry of intercession on our behalf in the presence of the Father. This does not imply any reluctance on the part of God to hear our prayers or to have mercy upon us. But it does mean that Christ has eternally united himself to humanity and that he has taken our humanity into the presence of God. Moreover, it means that Christ is the means of our approach to God, the one through whom we can come to God in prayer (John 14:12-14; 15:16; 16:23-24; Heb. 4:14-16). It means that through the ascension of Christ, the devil, the one who stood before the throne of God accusing our brethren day and night, has been cast down to earth (Rev. 12: 10; Job 1-2). This means that no one can lay anything to the charge of God's elect because it is God who justifies, because it is Christ who died, who rose again, and who is on the right hand of God interceding on our behalf (Rom. 8:33-34).

How does the sacrifice of Christ on Calvary over nineteen hundred years ago become effective for our salvation today?

The sacrifice of Christ becomes effective *for* us only as it becomes effective *in* us.

His death upon Calvary was an objective, unique, once-for-all historical event. Everything depends upon the fact that it is a deed that really happened, not just an abstract idea existing only in the mind of a thinking subject. Nevertheless, we must steadfastly reject any one-sided emphasis upon the atonement as a once-for-all historical event apart from the response of faith which brings the cross into the sphere of our everyday lives, making his cross our cross. Likewise to be repudiated with equal forcefulness is the opposite extreme, a one-sided emphasis upon our subjective experience of dying and rising with Christ without a due recognition that we can die and rise with him only because long ago on Calvary in an unique event wrought out in time and space he died for us. Avoiding the Scylla of an extreme objectivism (as in Barth) on the one hand and the Charybdis of an extreme subjectivism (as in Bultmann) on the other, we must steer a middle course, holding the objective and subjective elements of the atonement in indissoluble union.

Christ died *for* our sins, but he died for our sins in order that we might die *to* our sins. He went to the cross not in order that we might escape the cross but in order that we might take up our cross and follow him. His sacrifice of perfect obedience does not make our sacrifice of obedience unnecessary. Rather it makes it possible. Christ lived the life of the Servant of the Lord and he died in fulfilment of that ideal. He girded himself with a towel and washed his disciples' feet. He said, "I am among you as one who serves" (Luke 22:27). The principle of sacrifice and service by which he lived is that by which we are to live. "A disciple is not above his teacher, nor a servant above his master; it is enough for the disciple to be like his teacher, and the servant like his master" (Matt. 10:24-25). Not only are we to die to self that we might live unto him, but we are to give ourselves in the service of others that through us his Servant ministry may be extended in the world (Col. 1:24). But any thing which we do for him is based upon and determined by that which he has already done for us.

Apart from his sacrifice for us we dare not approach the righteous and holy God. But when by faith we make his sacrifice for our sins the medium of our approach to God, his death for us issues in his life in us (Rom. 5:10). The crucified Saviour meets us as the resurrected Lord. We are saved by grace through faith (Eph. 2:8), but the faith which issues in salvation is the faith which unites us to Christ in death and resurrection. His cross then becomes our cross, and his resurrection our resurrection (Gal. 2:20).

This is the individualistic aspect of the atonement. But just as in the proper interpretation of the atonement objective and subjective elements meet, even so in the correct understanding of the doctrine there is a harmonious blending of the individualistic and corporate aspects. God's purpose in the world is the establishment of his sovereignty in the lives of people who gladly recognize his Lordship. He accomplishes this through mighty acts of redemption. In the Old Testament era it was redemption from Egypt and the establishment of a covenant people. In the New Testament period it is the Christ-event and the establishment of a new covenant people, the church.

In the Christ-event the Creator takes the form of the creature; the Sovereign lives his life in space and time in the lowly ministry of the Servant. And the status of Lordship is conferred upon him, not as a prize of military conquest, but because of his sacrifice of perfect obedience, obedience unto death, even the death of the cross (Phil. 2:5-11). His resurrection and ascension are the necessary prelude to the sending of the Spirit.

The nucleus of the new covenant community was formed through the Servant ministry of Jesus. This new community was vitalized by Easter and empowered by Pentecost to become the witness concerning God's mighty act of redemption in history through Jesus Christ. "And we are witnesses to all that he did . . ." (Acts 10:39). "For we cannot but speak of what we have seen and heard" (Acts 4:20). And through the Spirit-empowered witness of this new covenant community other believers are called forth to be witnesses concerning the salvation of God in Jesus Christ.

Jesus Christ is the only Mediator between God and man; but the new covenant community, the church, is the divinely appointed instrument for witness in the world. From this Spirit-filled, believing community the New Testament Scriptures were called forth. These Scriptures in turn supply the regulative standard for the *kerygma* for later generations of Christians who were not eye witnesses of the redemptive act of God in Christ but who nevertheless have been appointed by God as his witnesses in the world. Apart from this witness none of us would be partakers of this salvation.

Moreover, just as there was a corporate aspect to the Old Testament Servant ideal there is a corporate aspect to the New Testament fulfilment. The church is in the world to continue the Servant ministry of the crucified and risen Saviour. The church is always subject to the temptation to demonic self-exaltation. Too often what the world sees is a power-hungry, secularized institution, rather than the hands and feet, eyes, ears, and mouth of the Lord — the body of Christ — giving itself in sacrificial service for the world, even as Christ, the Head, did in the days of his flesh.

The church as the body of Christ is the believing, witnessing community in which the redemptive act of God in Christ is proclaimed through word and ordinances. The ordinances, baptism and the Lord's Supper, are the word in pictorial form. Through them the sacrifice of Christ on our behalf and our union with him are graphically portrayed. Baptism depicts in dramatic symbolism Christ's death for us and our death and resurrection with him (Rom. 6:3-4; Col. 2:12). As the initiatory rite of the Christian faith it signifies our incorporation into Christ and into his body of which he is the Head (I Cor. 12:12-13). The Lord's Supper, which unlike baptism is to be repeated again and again, commemorates Christ's death for us in the past, acknowledges his presence with us in the present, and expresses the hope of the consummation of his salvation in us in the future (I Cor. 11:23-26; 10:16; Mark 14:25). It is not a re-offering of the sacrifice of Christ. This sacrifice was made once-for-all on Calvary, and by its very nature it is unrepeatable. Nevertheless, the Lord's Supper received in faith becomes a medium of our participation in the sacrifice made once-for-all, and it signifies on our part the renewal of the covenant and our solemn pledge to live as members of his body and fulfill his Servant ministry in the world.

These two ordinances are meaningless apart from faith on the part of the one who receives them. When received by faith they proclaim not only the sacrifice of Christ but our participation in that sacrifice as well.

Index of Subjects

Index of Authors

Scripture Index

Cover design by Cathy Culpepper Harvey
based on a work by Michelangelo